Dressing Dolls

IN

NINETEENTH CENTURY FASHIONS

"NO ROSE WITHOUT A THORN"

Dressing Dolls

In

Nineteenth Century Fashions

Albina Bailey

Library of Congress Catalog Card No. 74-29003
ISBN-0-87069-275-5

Drawings by the Author

Printed in the United States of America

Cover Design by Paul Davis

EDITOR'S NOTE:
As an aid to the reader quoted material has been set in
Bodoni Book type face and the author's comments have
been sent in Press Roman.

Wallace-Homestead Book Co.
580 Water's Edge Road
Lombard, Illinois 60148

DEDICATION

To all my Doll friends,
To you who Create, Love
and dress Dolls
And give so many a world
of Happiness

CONTENTS

PART I

PART II

PART III

ACKNOWLEDGEMENTS

My sincere thanks to my many wonderful doll friends who urged me to compile this book about dressing dolls in the lovely fashions of the nineteenth century. I am especially indebted to June Andrew's letters of encouragement as I compiled the material from my collection of "Peterson", "Godey", and "Delineator" magazines.

Rosaleen, another dear friend, is a member of a historical society. The members of her society have sewn replicas of 1860's dresses which they wear when participating in celebrations of historical events. I have a picture of Rosaleen dressed in one of her beautiful creations which helped to convince me of the importance of sharing this information.

Many precious hours have been divided between household duties and my love for dolls, sewing, and writing. My family has my heartfelt thanks for being so very understanding of my work.

FOREWORD

As the title of this book implies, all comments regarding fashion, material, color, and care of fabrics refer to the nineteenth century.

In order to choose substitutes for materials mentioned in the old text and since similar fabrics with modern names are often available, a Glossary of Nineteenth Century Terms has been included.

Many dollers like to use old fabrics to dress old dolls; however, when such material is not available the only alternative is to find a suitable substitute. These fashions can also be used with homemade cloth dolls as well as old dolls.

If I were asked to name my favorite fashion year, I would be unable to make a choice, for to me each period has a sparkle all its own. In fact, as I read and worked with these fashion books I began to feel as though I were living in the nineteenth century. Many times my letters to doll friends were accidentally dated 1873 rather than 1973. This was just one of the little mishaps which became my own personal comedy.

I hope you will enjoy reading these excerpts written in the literary style of another day. Happy Dolling to each of you. May you spend many pleasurable hours in dressmaking for your dolls.

—Albina Bailey

INTRODUCTION

As the bicentennial year of our nation approaches, many of us have become more aware of our country's rich heritage. We find ourselves searching our past for greatness and perhaps looking ahead with new confidence. Many among us will be interested in duplicating old fashions for use in various celebrations. Some may wish to use these patterns of the past century since only a very few Americans are fortunate enough to own apparel from those earliest years. Those who do are often understandably reluctant to subject such treasures to the possible ravages of a parade or other public gathering. Time, humidity, and moths have already done enough to render frail these delicate old things.

Stepping into this breach, Albina Bailey opens for us the pages of the foremost fashion periodicals of the 1850s through the 1870s. By sharing her experience as a seamstress, as well as her knowledge of the basic construction of these sometimes complicated garments, she has rendered a true service to her readers.

Doll collectors will surely applaud her efforts; the patterns she has redrawn will fit the average ten-inch mannequin. Seamstresses whose job it is to stitch up costumes for 1976 celebrants will appreciate the careful instructions. The author's notes give added insight for substituting modern fabrics to retain an authentic appearance. The "collections" shown at the end of each section offer additional ideas for the adventurous. In addition, a glossary defines the obscure terms used so often in the quoted material.

Altogether, this volume seems to me a most useful addition to the library shelf of those who sew for dolls or people.

—Johana Gast Anderton

PART I

* *
AUTHOR'S NOTE:
"GODEY'S" 1859

Nineteenth century styles changed frequently; in fact, the fabrics, colors, and trims seemed to change from month to month. Surah silks were used year round. Substitutes are easily found for surah as well as the velvets, satins, lawns, taffetas, and other widely used fabrics of the period. Beads, chenille, fringe, and a vast collection of trims are now available in modern department stores.

Crinoline is also available; however, for doll clothes pelon works up nicely as a substitute for interlinings, facings, and petticoats. Suitable laces are abundant in all widths and designs. A crocheted, tatted, knitted, or embroidered design on net is excellent for trimmings and edges.

A shoe diagram is given as it appears in the "Peterson" and "Godey" books for each decade. The shoes are simple to make and although intended for infants, they will fit the large modern dolls such as Pollyanna, Chatty Cathy, Penny Play-Pal, Charmin Chatty, or Toodles. For smaller dolls, sew the seams deeper to reduce the size.

The material quoted from the pages of the old fashion periodicals provide a special insight into the styles and frills of that century as well as an occasional glimpse of the mores and thought processes of the period.

* *

JANUARY 1859 GODEY

On black silk dresses, black checquered or embossed velvet is used in bands for quilles and the corsage; black velvet buttons and waist bands. Black silks, whether plain or in robes, are still considered the most ladylike walking-dresses for the street, and in fact the most serviceable dresses for universal wear. Plain poplins of dark brown and maroon, are favorites for the street.

The small cloth jackets or Zouave basques, as they are sometimes called, are trimmed in military style, with bands of cord across the front, terminating in tassels on each side. The elongated points in front have tassels to correspond.

Bodies of dresses are often cut high, the straight way of the cloth, round in front with a belt, and buckle placed at one side, or exactly in front, as may please the fancy.

Sleeves are almost universally wide and square. For dresses intended only for the house, two puffs, gathered into a band or cuff at the wrist, are made. The first puff serves as a cap; the other is long and full, reaching to the wrist. There is another close sleeve cut into a single piece, almost close to the arm at top and bottom, and very full over the elbow. A jockey at the top, and turned-up cuff at the bottom, take away from the extreme plainness.

FEBRUARY 1859 GODEY

A hood or talma for evening wear should be of some bright tint, mixed with white. Grosseille is the favorite shade this season; blue, rose-pink, and scarlet are also worn. Either of these colors as a ground, with a border of the mixed gray, black, and white, known as "chinchilla", and having the effect of that fur at a little distance is very desirable. There are many fanciful and graceful styles in shapes, decoration, etc. Hoods of silk, with quilted satin linings, bordered by ruches of ribbon, plaited closely, or in frills, are by some considered more elegant for the Opera or Concert room.

Plaid velvets are worn for evening dresses, both plain and embossed; but the importation is not large, the material being so costly. Brazilian moires, steel tissues, and several fancy silks, intended for dinner or evening dresses; a white silk with stripes of mallow-color satin representing very deep coques, surrounded by small rings in relief; a moire antique, of a white ground, flowered with pansies; another, covered with natural roses of all shades; a green moire, with a sprinkling of small black bouquets; another, with a black ground and a sprinkling of orange-color daisies; velvet pekins, Armures, plain velvets, Indian damasks; silks of all shades, with a sprinkling of very slight flowers, black on dark colors, white on light ones; a white ground, almost covered with very small black velvet crosses—this pattern may be had of any color; and, lastly, as a novelty of great richness and originality, an orange-color silk, with pattern flounces of black Astrakan and white plush velvet; all of which we may be interested to read of, though they range above our prescribed marks of simplicity in attire and economy in expenditure.

Velours de laine, terry velvet, plain or with velvet ribs, which last article is a novelty of the present year; then reps, especially brown and gold, and gray and black.

Among the fancy trimmings, for cloaks, mantles, and dresses, are silk thistles, a tassel pendant, mixed with jet or steel, bias pieces, plaits, crochet insertions, galloons, ruches, chenille plaits, velvet ruches, with lace and fringe. There is also a new kind of frog trimmings, fastened on each shoulder by a knot with several tassels, and sweeping across the breast in a handsome curve; the fourragere, of which we gave a description some time ago, is in the same style, but thicker and heavier; and various ornaments, embellished and complicated in a thousand ways; one of them in particular, with a black openwork gallery, plaid arcades, and twisted plaid fringe.

The making of dresses has certainly become much less complicated. Bodies for walking costumes are nearly all made high and plain, without other ornament than a pretty row of buttons, or a few bows, and are confined round the waistband with a buckle.

Sleeves are now closed at the wrist, and have a cuff trimmed with velvet or with ruches of ribbons. On dresses intended for visiting or evening dress, we see a berthe or draperies; two flounces, sometimes, with a figured pattern; or, when they are plain, surmounted by other smaller flounces. The sleeves of these dresses are still made open very wide, and very long.

MARCH 1859 GODEY

According to the present fashion, dresses may be made with one skirt trimmed with flounces or with quilles, or they may have two skirts. In the latter case, when the dress is composed of organdy or any other light fabric, the skirts may be edged with a bouillonne, through which a running of ribbon is passed. The corsage is sometimes ornamented with a fichu of the same material as the dress, trimmed round with a bouillonne.

APRIL 1859 GODEY

The materials of the season are the "Shilling calicoes" of our New England friends, which are almost as handsome if not so fine or so wide, as the English and French chintzes close beside them; the same neat patterns, buff, pink, pale-green, stone-colored, and white grounds, and small patterns in bright colors. Scotch ginghams, chine, striped, or in plain cheques, are admirable for colors and texture this season. Chambrays, plain-colored lawns, printed jaconets, brilliants, and Marseilles are all of them suited to children's dresses and morning or house dresses for any lady, married or single. The spring silks for street dress have favorite shades, or rather two shades of favorite colors in alternate narrow Bayadere stripes, chine patterns, and square cheques, or, rather blocks. Among the colors, pale sea-green, bright Pomona, or apple-green, a delicate shade of mauve, called dahlia-color by some, though it is the true grosielle or gooseberry; the pink most in favor is the lightest shade of the crimson worn the past fall, under this family name, and is called Alpine rose; pale-blue, buff, all the drabs, silver and white, and the delicate shade of fawn and tan known as hazel-nut, the most springlike of all russets, which, in reality, belong to autumn. The description of the lighter fabrics, which come chiefly in pattern dresses, known as robes a deux jupes, robes a volant, robes a princess, robes a lez, etc., as their style may be.

JUNE 1859 GODEY

The skirts are worn plain, double, triple, tunic fashion, and with two flounces, in the latter case, the upper one is set into the waist, and has the effect of a double skirt.

The corsages are plain, with a short, rather blunt point before and behind, with surplus folds, and a fichu, or any style of berthe or bretelle that may be fancied, or as the plate which accompanies each robe directs. The round corsage, with belt and buckle, is chiefly worn; it may be cut square, or opened partially for a chemisette at the throat. The sleeves are chiefly in puffs and straight flounces; sleeves closed at the wrist are not suitable for summer, except for morning or traveling dress.

SEPTEMBER 1859 GODEY

No later than last summer the white body and colored skirt were considered excessively bad taste, and English ladies who preferred comfort to fashion, and still persisted in the mode of dress, were thought unpardonably old-fashioned. Now they are considered very novel. We are sure that those of our readers who look to economy in that frightfully large item of a lady's expense, dress, will be glad of the accession to power of the Zouave, as it is an excellent way of using up skirts of dresses whose bodies alone have suffered wear. To those more fortunate ones who have not to consider this, it will also be acceptable as a pretty, becoming, and above all, fashionable mode of dress.

Small flounces, set on in groups of two or three, with plain spaces between them, a fashion introduced to cover the very plain look of a single barege or organdy skirt the past summer, will be retained for the lighter silks purchased by the yard, while in robes deep flounces and double skirts will continue to be worn, though this is probably their last season.

The effort to establish an anti-crinoline movement has been futile, though the prime movers say that they will succeed as winter begins. The fact is, the light dresses require some support, and the crinoline is just the article to give it that, without causing the wearer the inconvenience from the heat that the jupons empeses always occasion. There is something stately in the set of a heavy silk or velvet dress, as it falls in rich and graceful folds, and crinoline there would seem out of place; but for flounces we must still preserve the unfortunate garment which meets with so much disdain from the gentlemen.

As to colors the admixture of black with everything is the rage. It is extremely becoming in contrast with bright colors to a brunette, and may be judiciously employed so as to add still greater delicacy to a blonde. Black silk dresses, if considered too sombre, may be lighted by the introduction of cherry, scarlet, green, or blue into the fringe or ribbon employed as trimming, even flame-color; and the bright orange of the nasturtium is used here, as well as for bonnets.

Young and old no longer insist upon displaying the figure in a Raglan Sacque. The graceful, flowing outline of the pointed and rounded burnous are much more likely to be generally becoming. We cannot praise too highly the perfect good taste and elegance of a garment of this style of fine light ladies cloth, a delicate shade of ashes of roses, a shade that combines the livelier tint with pure coolness of gray. When the burnous was extremely ample in the skirt, though plaited in at the back in such a way as to fall lightly to the figure. A hood, known best as the Riding Hood, from being seen in the pictures of the favorite little nursery heroine, rounded to the shoulder and was finished by a ruche of quilled velvet ribbon (black), an inch or more in width, and ornamented by two rich tassels in silk and chenille. A ruche of quilled velvet surrounded the burnous headed by a row of plain velvet ribbon set on flat at a little distance.

Algerine cloth, a woollen material at once thick and light in gray, drab, etc., chequed and striped with black, will be made into these indispensable neglige outer garments. All the shades of tan and russet, especially tan d'or, are manufactured, with many varieties of shape and trimming, for fall wear; and importations of guipure and crochet ornaments promise richness and elegance for the cloths and velvets of approaching winter.

NOVEMBER 1859 GODEY

Bonnets are considerably larger than we have been accustomed to of late; the shape of the brim, flat across the top, and widening at the ears; the crowns are in every variety, soft, folded, square, plain, every fancy may be suited. The newest feathers are long ostrich plumes, with marabout tips, slightly rolled, or curved to fall with grace. There is a great choice in feathers, however, as in crowns, from a cock's plume to the pure ostrich, singly, in tufts, and coquilles.

DECEMBER 1859 GODEY

The narrow flounces are seen more and more, nor should we be surprised if they succeeded double skirts by spring, when all thin materials will look charmingly in these narrow ruffles, that recall the patient labor of our grandmothers, in their yards of hemming. The sewing-machine will have full employment, and outdo even this traditionary industry; the heading of flounces is a part of their present phase, they have been so long set on with a cord. Many group and graduate them; others prefer to have "all thirty" of the same width. We shall have more to say of this next month.

The favorite materials for walking dresses are poplins—Irish, French, plain and figure-ottoman velvets and reps. These materials, being so heavy, do not admit of much trimming. Bands of velvet, embossed velvet ribbons, and fringes with velvet headings are the most suitable applications. Guipure lace and crochet ornaments are not out of place with them. Deep blue and black, green, purple, brown, crimson, currant, and scarlet, with black, in figures and stripes, prevail. There are few cheques worn on these heavier goods, except the wide, broad plaids, that are unsuited to small figures.

Medium silks were never so cheap as now; there is a large choice in silks. Bayadere horizontal stripes being the general style. The alternate stripe being black. For morning-dresses, the printed cashmere robes are very elegant, deep garland border, and fine bouquets scattered through the centre on a purple, blue, maroon, grosielle, green or black ground. Very pretty all-wool mousselines and cashmeres have spots, stars, acorns, wheat-ears, bouquets, etc., in all the bright shades, on the same colored grounds. Printed French merinos are also in this style, and are extremely suitable for children's wear.

The Zouave jacket may be made in black cloth or velvet, for home wear, with skirts whose waists have "out-lived their usefulness". They are especially suitable with dark silks, and a waist of this kind with a black silk skirt will do any amount of street service. Black silk are trimmed with a combination of black and crimson, black and purple, etc., when intended for dress occasions.

In bonnets there are many little novelties, as the winter advances. There is a new veil, called the clotilde, which is of itself almost a full trimming for any bonnet. They are nearly oblong in shape, with a circular opening to admit the crown; the rounded front covers the brim, and the back piece, or curtain, falls over the cape of the hat, and caught up on each side by sprays of flowers, or a tasteful knot of ribbons. The most elegant velvet needs no ornament, when the veil is of real chantilly.

NOTES AND QUERIES

New colors for dresses, etc: The names given refer to new shades of well-known colors, a brown, purple, crimson, etc. Every season brings a new tint, which is known by a new name, that is all. Grosielle, as we have often explained, is gooseberry; China aster, Alpine pansy, Gilly flower, Alpine current, etc., are only different shades of red and purple. We have a new green, blue, and pink, with every Spring, as Azoff green, Leveres' pink, Eugenie blue.

STORAGE OF SILK

Silk articles should not be kept in white paper, as the chloride of lime in bleaching paper will probably impair the color of the silk. Brown or blue paper is better, and the yellowish, smooth India paper is best of all. Silks intended for dresses should not be kept long in the house before they are made up, as lying in the folds will have a tendency to impair its durability, by causing it to cut or split, particularly if the silk has been thickened by gum. Dresses of velvet should not be laid by with any weight on them, for if the nap of thin velvet is laid down, it is not possible to raise it again. Hard silk should never be wrinkled, because the thread is easily broken in the creases, and it never can be rectified. The way to take the wrinkles out of the silk scarfs and handkerchiefs is to moisten the surface evenly with a spoon and some wheat glue, and then pin the silk with some toilet-pins around the shelves or on a mattress or feather bed, taking pains to draw out the silk as soon as possible; when dry, the

ROBE IMPERATRICE, WITH ZOUAVE JACKET.

The material is a delicate buff cambric, with designs in a rich chocolate brown.

(From the celebrated establishment of Messrs. A. T. STEWART & Co., *of New York.)*

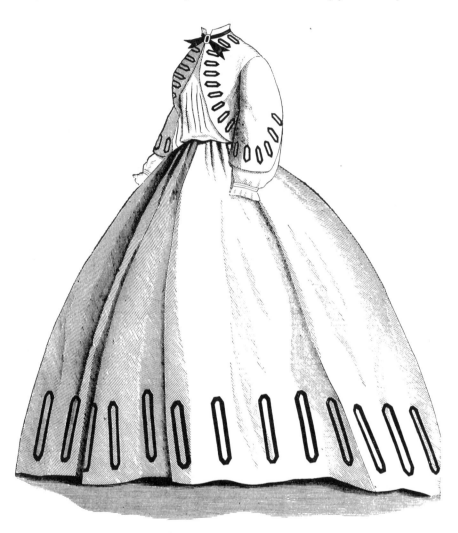

wrinkles will have disappeared. It is a nice job to dress light-colored silk, and few should try it. Some silk articles should be moistened with weak glue or gum-water, and the wrinkles ironed out with a hot flat-iron on the wrong side.

MECHLIN LACE

We confess to a partiality for this delicate and lady-like point, so much in use for the abundant frills that surround the faces, and shade the fair necks of those old family beauties, known to us only by their portraits.

In former days Mechlin was renowned for its lace manufactures. For a century and more it held supremacy in the markets of Europe, and the Mechlin lace was considered the perfection of that article, commanding by far the highest prices, and being the source of a large revenue to its fabricators. It has, however, fallen off very considerably of late years, in supply and demand. While this lace is not so fine as that which is made at Brussels, it is much more durable, and, therefore, of more intrinsic value as an article of use. In regard to lace not produced by hand, that which is known as bobbin-net may be said to surpass every other branch of human industry in the complex ingenuity of its machinery; one of the "spotting frames", as they are termed being as much beyond the most curious chronometer, in multiplicity of mechanical device, as that is beyond a common hand-saw.

* * * * * * * * * * * * * * * * * * *

AUTHOR'S NOTE:

I find it so interesting to know how silks, velvets, and other fabrics were cared for and stored. This answers our question of how the beautiful fashions of another day have come to our museums in such excellent condition.

With this information on restoring silk, old wrinkled silk pieces which may have been laid away can now be taken out and put in useable condition.

* * * * * * * * * * * * * * * * * * *

EMBROIDERY DESIGNS TAKEN FROM "GODEY" 1859

FOR CHEMISE YOKES AND REVERS

BRAIDING PATTERN

INSERTION

FOR A BREAKFAST CAP

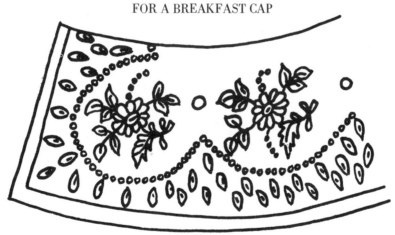

LATEST STYLE OF COLLAR

PATTERN FOR SILK OR MUSLIN EMBROIDERY

EMBROIDERY ON FLANNEL

EMBROIDERY FOR CHEMISE

EMBROIDERY FOR FLANNEL OR MERINO

EMBROIDERY FOR A MUSLIN SKIRT

DESIGN FOR SILK EMBROIDERY

1859 GODEY
A GRAND SELECTION OF SLEEVES

Fig. 1.   Simple undersleeve for home wear, closed at the wrist. Plain Swiss muslin, with a narrow ribbon drawn through the wristband.

Fig. 1

Fig. 2.   Dotted muslin, with puffs, and a ribbon drawn through.

Fig. 2

Fig. 3.   Sleeve for street or dinner dress. It is composed of net and Valenciennes lace, the cuff is deep, and disposed in wings or points overlapping.

Fig. 3

Fig. 4.   Sleeve of wrought muslin and lace. The sleeve has two puffs of plain muslin and a flounce of embroidery edged with lace, caught up on the forearm with a bow of some delicate shade.

Fig. 5

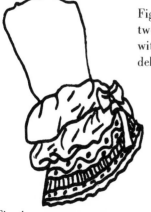

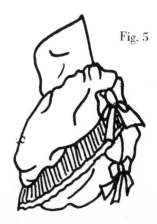

Fig. 4

Fig. 5.   Undersleeve with frill of lace and two puffs of net or muslin; close at the wrist; finished by bows on the forearm.

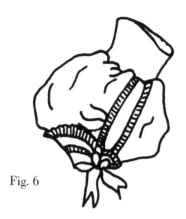

Fig. 6

Fig. 6. Swiss muslin undersleeve for mourning; it may also be made in Tarletan, or net, and is an excellent pattern. On the forearm, and around the cuff is a puff through which a black ribbon is drawn, which is fastened by a bow at the wrist.

Fig. 7. Extremely neat and popular made of plain linen, cambric, or muslin, plaided with a narrow black velvet ribbon. Satin ribbon of any hue may be used; the velvet will answer for all purposes and colors in the dress. Very suitable for Fall and Winter wear.

Fig. 7

Fig. 8. Sleeve of white Brussels net, crossed by bands of black velvet, and edged with black lace; pretty for winter wear.

Fig. 8

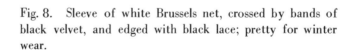

Fig. 9. Cambric sleeve, delicately embroidered.

Fig. 9

1859 GODEY
TRIMMING FOR PETTICOATS IN BRODERIE ANGLAISE

MATERIALS: Fine muslin; No. 24 Cotton. This pattern, unique as it is, will be found to have a very rich effect. Care should be taken to make all points of the scallop very clear and even. Then one side of the leaf is formed of holes cut out and worked over; and the other is outlined in scallops of buttonhole stitch, with small eyelet-holes pierced and sewed over within them, to give lightness to this part of the leaf. A thread being held in, in all the sewing over, adds much to the wear of embroidery.

EMBROIDERY FOR UNDERCLOTHES

FOR CHAIN STITCH OR BRAIDING

TRIMMING FOR PETTICOATS

1859 GODEY
LADIES DRAWERS

Two favorite styles of trimmings for the pantalettes; the first
is gathered into a band of cambric embroidery, which is edged
by a frill.

The second has a hem, straight band of inserting, and frill.
They may also be tucked in groups, or simply embroidered on
the edge.

EMBROIDERY FOR CHEMISE

FOR CHEMISE BAND

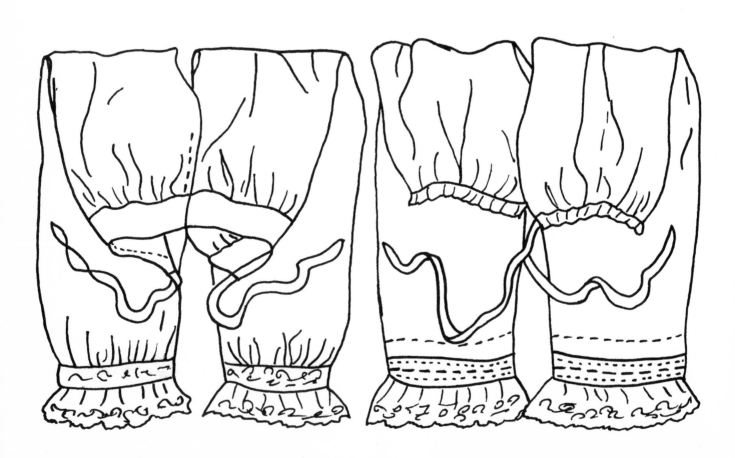

"FIRST DRAWERS"   "SECOND DRAWERS"

FRONT VIEW

BACK VIEW

1859 GODEY
THE MATINEE SKIRT

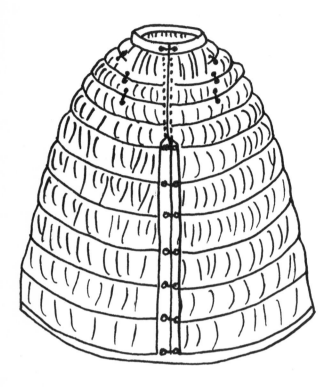

insert the catch and turn it down, so that it lies along the edged centre of the slide. Draw the fullness of the muslin evenly over the hoops; and to do this, it may be necessary to have the skirt on a hook, so that it may readily be turned around. The hoops of the Adjustable Bustle and the cord at the bottom are not to be removed for washing.

TO ADJUST THE PATENT BUSTLE: The lacings go at the back of the person, and by drawing or slackening them, the size is increased or diminished. It is advisable to adjust the bustle, and properly secure the lace when the skirt is first worn, regard being first had to the spring of the basque, as nothing looks worse than to see the basque lie light over the skirts. For wet weather, however, it is a good plan to increase the size of the Bustle, the better to keep the skirts out of the mud.

* *
AUTHOR'S NOTE:

This matinee skirt should be easy to make since it lies flat before the hoops are added. Hoops may be made by cutting circular strips from a large bleach bottle. These will insert easily in the tapes; or you may choose to purchase ready-made boning for the hoops.

* *

DIRECTIONS FOR USING: Every wearer of Skeleton Hoop Skirts has experienced more or less inconvenience and danger from the hoops catching in everything that came in their way—entangling the feet in ascending stairs, the steps of an omnibus, etc.—and has only continued to patronize them, because it was so troublesome to remove and replace the hoops of the muslin skirts for the purpose of washing. The Matinee Skirt, made of fine muslin, with 11 hoops and the adjustable Bustle, combines all the advantages of the former muslin and skeleton skirts, with this great additional one, that by means of the Patent Detachable Hoop Fastening, the hoops can be removed and replaced instantly and easily. The muslin skirt will cost no more for washing than an ordinary over-skirt, and the cut of the garment will insure its graceful set on the person. The band down the front is stitched on one side and hooked on the other, covering the Patent Detachable Fastening.

TO REMOVE THE HOOPS: Unhook the band down the front and detach each hoop by turning up the small wire catching and drawing it out, by which the hoops can be taken from the slide. When all the fastenings are thus detached, lay the skirt flat on a table and withdraw the hoops.

TO REPLACE THE HOOPS: Again lay the muslin flat on the table and run in all the hoops. Fasten each by slipping one end into the slide, and then the other over it, each end being flush with one extremity of the slide. The small holes through which the catch is to go will form a tube, in which

1859 GODEY
SHOE FASHIONS DESCRIPTIONS

For walking dress, kid boots, buttoned at the side, and with small heels. The kid may be either black or colored. Gray and bronze color are extremely fashionable.

For ball dress, satin slippers, white or colored, or white satin boots, or silk boots to match the color of the robe.

Morning slippers are made of kid, morocco, velvet, satin, and various fancy materials. They are frequently ornamented with embroidery in colored silks or gold and silver thread, and are trimmed with ruches of ribbon, fringe, and passementerie.

TWO STYLES OF SHOES

1859 GODEY
HAIR-NET IN CHENILLE AND BEADS

These hair-nets are made in many varieties of materials; beads, gold and silver thread, course netting-silk, and many in a chenille, manufactured for ornamental purposes, which has a slight wire inserted in its centre, which enables it to retain any form required. We have given in our illustration a centre formed of chenille and beads. Our space not permitting us to give the full size, it is merely necessary to enlarge it by repeating the outer rows until it is sufficiently expanded. The beads used must be large enough to allow the chenille to pass through them. It is formed by linking the chenille through and through, leaving the loops of the length required to form the pattern given. The ornamental centre is formed separately, the outer part being worked round it until it is the right size. When completed an elastic is threaded through the last row of loops which confines it round the head, and encloses the back hair when dressed low down at the back of the neck.

* * * * * * * * * * * * * * * * * * * *

AUTHOR'S NOTE:
The hair-net will work up nicely with the "craft chenille" sold at hobby shops. The size illustrated is a good size for a doll. If you prefer a larger or smaller net, reduce or enlarge by adding more loops as described. A smaller size net may be made by ending with the inner ring, rather than the outer rim as shown in drawing.

* * * * * * * * * * * * * * * * * * * *

1859 GODEY
APPLIQUE RETICULE

There is hardly anyone who does not occasionally stand in need of a bag, at once pretty and commodious; and as the style of design we now give certainly combines these qualities we hope it will be generally popular. There are several modes of working the sides, which are intended to be rather stiff. Either the pattern may be cut or stamped on, and one piece of cloth or leather, and applique with thin gum to another, the outlines being covered by a row of braid; or the pattern may be marked and simply braided, on either materials; or it may be marked on canvas, and worked in two colors, in cross-stitch with a line of gold-colored silk stitches by way of outline. A thin card-board should be introduced between the outer part and the lining, to make the side firm.

To make up this bag, unite the sides by a strip of the silk, three or four inches in width. It must be gathered at each edge, being very full. The side should be piped all round the edge with some of the same silk. The upper part, a straight piece of silk, is set on each side to the work, and half the silk-puffing joined up the sides, and then the lining, which comes from within the running, below the hem at the top, and goes down to the bottom, is added. The silk puffing must be lined separately. In putting on the silk top, lay it beneath the side, so that the form of the latter is preserved. Run in the cords and tassels to draw it up.

* * * * * * * * * * * * * * * * * * *

AUTHOR'S NOTE:

This is pretty made in the size illustrated. Trace pattern on tissue, cut two from cardboard, cover the cardboard with material of your choice, snipping where needed to fit well, glue edges to backside of cardboard. Trace the design onto the material, and textile paint, embroider, or cut a contrasting design from material and glue on to give the appliqued look as shown. Either way is pretty. Follow instructions for reticule and make the ruching much narrower in width for doll size. A narrow ribbon would also serve well for the ruching if it matches the material. Line all.

* * * * * * * * * * * * * * * * * * *

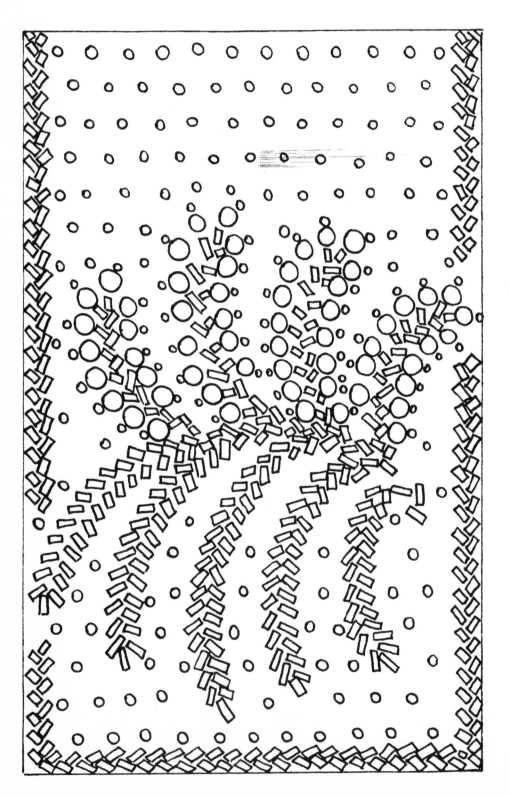

LAPPET FOR THE HAIR IN
BEADS AND BUGLES

1859 GODEY
LAPPET FOR THE HAIR IN BEADS AND BUGLES

It is quite certain that a lady's head should not be too elaborately ornamented; but there are now many graceful and becoming ornaments which add very much to the finish of a dress. Among these, perhaps the prettiest, is the lappet falling from the back of the hair. We have given a design for one which has a very pretty effect, and which any lady can execute with perfect ease. It is composed of either black or white net, and the pattern is formed of white bugles and pearl beads. The small border within a rather wide hem is entirely worked in small bugles, as well as the branches. Two sizes of the pearl beads are required, as will be seen in our illustration. It may be arranged to look equally well for mourning by substituting black bugles and black beads for the white. Two of these lappets, gathered in at the top with a bow of velvet and a simple white or red rose, with a few green leaves, forms a very elegant headdress for evening wear for ball or concert.

1859 GODEY
THE SELF SUPPORTING TOURNURE

That this invention should not have been made long ago is surprising, for it is very simple, and yet the very best article to give beauty to the human figure. All other devices to give rotundity to the shape betray themselves, while this yields to the figure and makes no sign of its existence in the gait of a lady. The light, plaint steel springs which proceed from the steel waistband, below or above the edge of it, as may be needed by short or long waists, perform their office admirably. These are represented by the vertical bands. The horizontal ones represent broad tapes, which sustain the general drapery. Nothing could be invented so well calculated to meet the demands of these who, in full dress, wish to present the realization of a well-shaped figure. This Tournure is now generally adopted by fashionable ladies in all parts of the country, and is prized because it never loses its ability to sustain and round the skirts, without suggesting that it is employed for such a purpose. The demand for it is great, but the large manufactory in this city will be able to supply every dress and millinery establishment in the country during the present season. Ladies will be delighted to throw away the cumberson articles hitherto used to improve the figure, and adopt this admirable invention, which has been patented.

JUNE 1859 GODEY
FICHU BERTHE AND DIAGRAM

We give again an engraving of how to make ones own dresses, and accompany them, as usual, with diagrams, by which they may be cut out. This is a beautiful Fichu Berthe, appropriate for the season, and such as any young lady can make for herself without difficulty. Nos. 1 and 2 of the diagram, when enlarged, will show how the fichu is to be cut. It is afterward to be trimmed with lace.

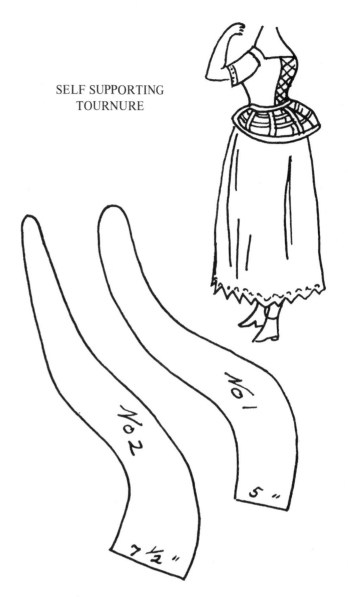

SELF SUPPORTING TOURNURE

FICHU BERTHE AND DIAGRAM (FITS A SMALL DOLL)

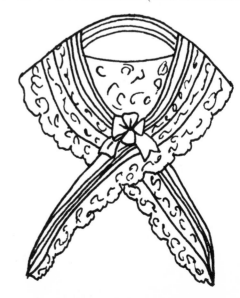

HINT

TO WASH LACE OR BLONDE: Valuable lace, or French blonde, may be washed with care, to look as well as new. Thread lace should be carefully taken off from any article to which it has been sewed; but blonde may be left attached to the quilling net. The lace must be wound round a smooth roller, or a common wine bottle filled with water, and covered with clean linen. This bottle should be placed upright, in a strong, cold lather of white soap and water, where it must remain on a warm hearth for a day or two, till all the dirt is drawn out of the lace, renewing the lather every day. When quite clean, it must be partly dried in the sun, upon the bottle, then taken off, and pinned out carefully upon a pillow, using a separate pin for every point or scollop. Let it remain till perfectly dry, when it may be unpinned and put away. It must not be starched or ironed.

* * * * * * * * * * * * * * * * * * *

AUTHOR'S NOTE:

I have given these lace washing instructions because many women own some lovely old laces which are quite soiled and need special care in washing. We should benefit by using this method of lace washing as it was used in 1859 to preserve old laces since ironing could ruin a treasured piece of lace.

A short time ago I was fortunate to find a shoe box of old lace sitting on the floor behind some picture frames in an antique shop. The lace is extremely discolored from dust and thick soil. This box of soiled lace is waiting to be washed and I plan to use the method given here in an attempt to preserve the lace and keep it from falling apart.

* * * * * * * * * * * * * * * * * * *

1859 GODEY
SOME NEW MATERIALS AND DESCRIPTIONS

We paid a visit to the extensive establishment of T.W. Evans & Co., one of the largest and best conducted drygoods stores we have ever seen. Everything that a lady's heart could desire in the shape of dress was scattered around us in profusion. We went "up stairs and down stairs", and exquisite fabrics met our eyes at every step.

Mr. Evans has just opened a full and complete assortment of all the newest materials for dresses that will be in demand for the coming year, from the richest silks to fabrics whose texture seemed suitable for Queen Titania to take an airing in.

Their traveling dress goods are of the newest style and materials, and manufactured expressly for their sales in English, German, and French markets. One was shown of a Pongee silk, of a delicate corn-color, to be trimmed with black velvet, and which will make a unique and elegant dress for a fair traveler. There is every variety in their stock, both in color and material.

From traveling dresses we turned to the counter where were displayed a new style of goods, the Barege Anglaise, Argentines, and Batiste de Laine. The goods vary from a thick-ness suitable to spring wear to a gauzy texture which will be refreshing on warm, oppressive July and August days. The Barege Anglaise possesses an advantage over the old barege goods, in having a silk cord interwoven, which gives it a certain stiffness, and prevents its clinging in the close, warm folds so objectionable in the common barege.

The stock of silks is very large, and comprising every variety to suit the most fastidious taste-rich ones, and from those to the lighter and more delicate kinds, for the warmer months.

The organdies and lawns are of the most exquisite patterns; some of them, as a lady friend of ours declared, looked "good enough to eat".

All dress goods, whether by the yard or in Robes a double Jupe, or Robes a deux Volants, will be found in their assortment. The only difficulty the fair purchasers will complain of will be how to choose, and so great a variety.

EMBROIDERY FOR A NIGHT CAP

1859 BABY'S FIRST SHOE
(WILL FIT DOLLS 20" - 24")

MATERIALS: One-eighth yard of fine flannel will make one pair of shoes. One yard white silk twist, or cotton embroidery thread. One and one-half yards narrow white ribbon for bows and ties.

This shoe is made in one piece. Trace the pattern on paper. Cut out the shape in brown or stout paper, taking care to mark the turnings. It will be as well to shrink the flannel first by pouring boiling water on it, and letting it stand till cold; afterwards dry and iron.

Double the paper patterns together; press down the turnings, double the flannel lengthwise, tack the paper pattern on the flannel, stitch up the backs, and stitch down the front from the notch in the turning to the toe, open the shoe, cut the flannel to the size of the turnings, and then take off the pattern; the heel and toe will then fit into its place, which must now be stitched; open the turnings of front and back, and tack them down, also the turning round the top and the slit. Then turn the shoe on the right side and work herring-bone, chain, or half-chain stitch, as in drawings, round the top and down the front, beginning at the back seam at the top, and work down to the toe. Then fasten off. Begin again at the back, and work down the other side to the toe; or, if herring-bone stitch, it may be worked continuously round without fastening off. Make four eyelet holes on each side to draw the ribbon. Then trim the shoes.

BABY'S FIRST SHOE

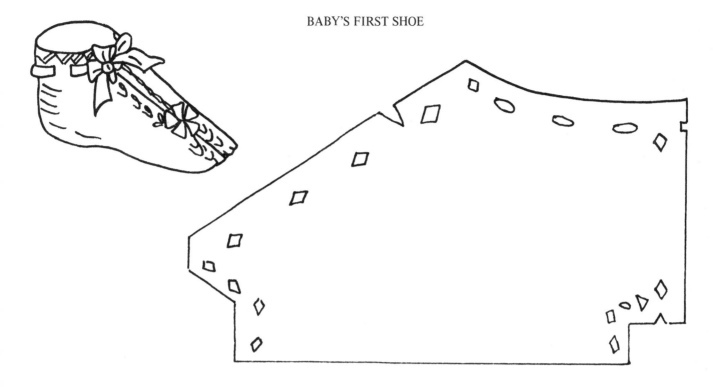

1859 GODEY
HONITON LACE SPRIG

We have much pleasure in supplying a genuine Honiton Lace sprig, which we have procured for the purpose. This is exactly what is used by the lace-makers, the same outline being pricked by them, and the sprig worked on the cushion with bobbins. This can be closely imitated by being sewn over on fine clear muslin, cut out, the centre filled with a lace stitch, and so fastened down on clear Brussels net. Worked in this way, the imitation is so close as not to be easily detected, more especially as the sprig we have given is perfectly genuine.

* * * * * * * * * * * * * * * * * * * *

AUTHOR'S NOTE:

If you draw this sprig design on paper and pin it under a piece of net, working the threads as shown in the drawing, with the thread of your choice, you will have a very authentic piece of lace for your doll dressing.

* *

* *

AUTHOR'S NOTE:

TRAVELING RETICULE

Make a band to fit doll's waist as shown in drawing. Interline the band with pelon or crinoline. Trace the beading design on material and bead with very small seed beads, or embroider if you prefer.

Using the drawing as a pattern, cut pelon or crinoline for interlining. Cut material of your choice for outer bag. (Note: When tracing the bag, add flap piece to the top of the reticule for the full pattern.) Trace the beadwork design on the material and work with seed beads or embroidery. Sew all together with very narrow seams (allow for seams when cutting), then line all. Sew hooks and eyes to back band, attach a tiny clasp to flap, and sew a snap under the flap for closing.

The clasp may be taken from an old piece of broken jewelry. Bracelets are sometimes attached by very small clasp openings which would be ideal for this purpose. Small earrings or necklaces may also have an attractive ornamental clasp which would prove suitable.

Since enamel jewelry was a fashionable accessory in the nineteenth century it might be wise to purchase new pieces of enamel jewelry at special discontinued sales to have on hand when the need arises for a doll accessory.

* *

TRAVELING RETICULE

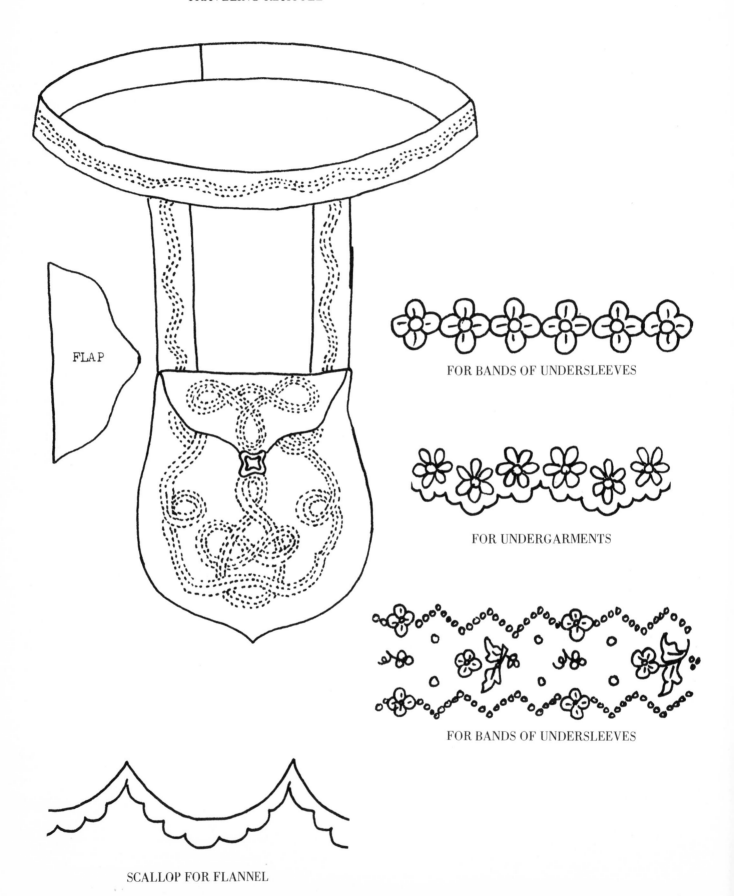

FLAP

FOR BANDS OF UNDERSLEEVES

FOR UNDERGARMENTS

FOR BANDS OF UNDERSLEEVES

SCALLOP FOR FLANNEL

**1859 GODEY
EMBROIDERY BORDER FOR A DRESS**

We give a design which has an especially good effect for any purpose where a rich border is required. It may be worked on either a thick or thin muslin. The holes are cut and worked round in buttonhole stitch; the large leaves at the bottom are filled in with point d'or. The borders at the top are worked in satin stitch. The proper cottons to use are Nos. 20 and 24.

MARCH 1859 GODEY
BALL OR PARTY DRESS
(FITS 10" MANNIKIN DOLLS)

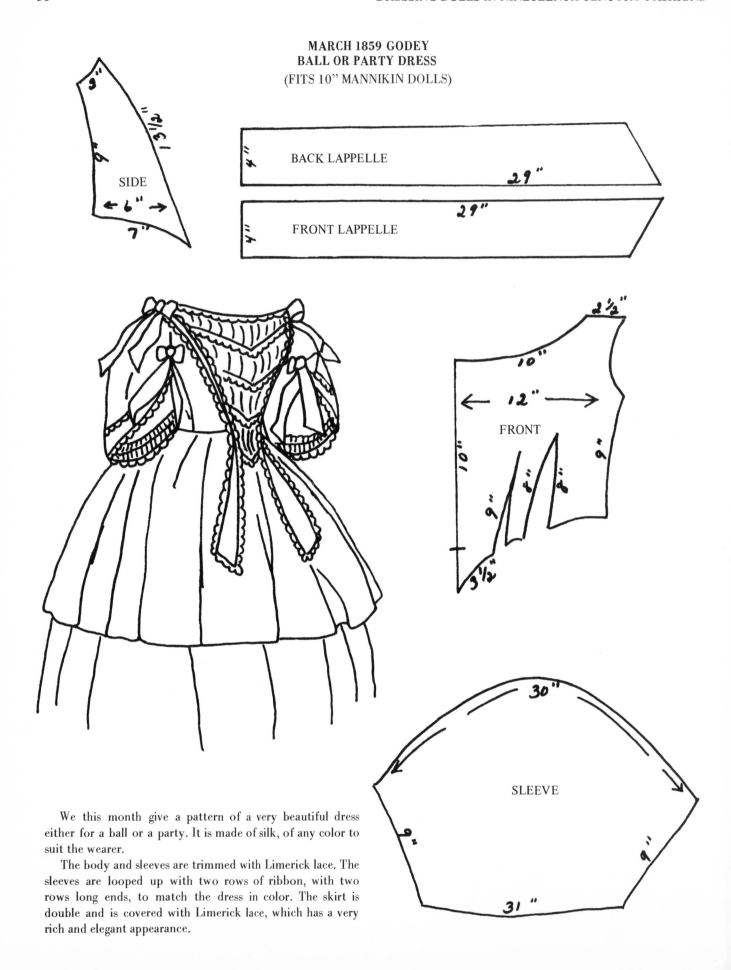

We this month give a pattern of a very beautiful dress either for a ball or a party. It is made of silk, of any color to suit the wearer.

The body and sleeves are trimmed with Limerick lace. The sleeves are looped up with two rows of ribbon, with two rows long ends, to match the dress in color. The skirt is double and is covered with Limerick lace, which has a very rich and elegant appearance.

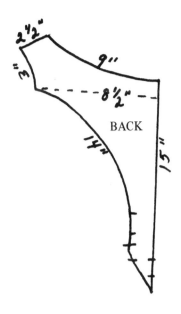

* * * * * * * * * * * * * * * * * * *
AUTHOR'S NOTE:

Cut material and lining of silk. I find a very good substitute for silk is sheath lining for the soft silks, and silk taffeta for the body silks.

BODICE

Sew darts in front bodice; sew back, side, and shoulder seams. Gather sleeves at armhole edge, sew sleeves to armholes, easing in to fit bodice armhole. Sew lace trim to sleeve as shown in drawing. Sew sleeve seam and side seams of bodice in one.

Sew lace trim to bodice front and neckline, shaping the trim to points at center front bodice. After lining bodice, make a ruching of gauze or net and sew to underpart of sleeve as shown in drawing.

Punch small holes in back bodice, using a small awl. Lace the closing with heavy buttonhole thread or very narrow cord to match the color of the material.

Sew lappets together at shoulder seams. Sew lace all around edges and line lappets. Catch stitch lappets at shoulders of bodice, narrowing to waistline and widening at bodice fronts at points of bodice as shown in drawing.

Cut two skirts, one full length and one half-length for over skirt. Cut both skirts 35" wide, and of a length necessary for the doll. Sew the two skirts together at waistline and narrowly pleat across to fit bodice waistline. Sew back seams. Cut a three inch facing for each skirt, sew these to each hemline, turn under and hem with blindstitch.

Sew the skirt to bodice waistline leaving the back and front points of bodice free of stitching. In other words, the skirt is sewed straight across bodice waistline. The front and back points are left loose for the appearance of a two-piece dress. Make small ribbon bows and sew to shoulders and sleeves as described earlier.

* *

RAPHAEL DRESS APRIL 1859 GODEY
(FITS 10" MANNIKIN DOLLS)

The skirt is double, the upper part being looped up, at regular intervals with plisse, passing from under the hem of the upper skirt to the waist.

With this dress is worn an underbody of fullings 7 insertion, either of lace, or muslin, having a pink silk lining, which displays the design of the lace or embroidery to great advantage, and contrasts well with the dress, which may be lighter or darker silk, according to taste.

* * * * * * * * * * * * * * * * * * *
AUTHOR'S NOTE:

BODICE

Sew back to side back. Sew front center to front sides. Sew shoulder seams front and back in diagonal position from X mark at neckline. Sew lining in same manner.

SLEEVE

Sew sleeve slashes together, gathering and shirring each to fit doll's arm and to resemble drawing. Sew the sleeve ruffle to lower part of sleeve, gathering to fit shirred sleeve. Sew sleeve to armholes, shirring to fit.

Using center front and side front pieces, from shoulders to dashlines on bodice, cut a piece of silk lining. Ruche small pieces of lace as shown at the neckline, sew onto the silk piece and sew buttons in the center. Sew this onto bodice to give the effect of an underbody. Sew velvet, satin, or ribbon of your choice to the sleeve ruffle, to the bodice front and back as shown in drawing, and to the lower part of bodice. Sew a lace ruffle to bodice waistline, or use a piece of silk. Line all.

Sleeve ruffle only is lined. Make a lace closing on back bodice by punching the holes with an awl and lacing with narrow cord.

SKIRT

Make this skirt using the directions given for Ball Dress, adding the ruching to the overskirt from hem to waistline. Hem each skirt with skirt facing. Add a waistband and close with hook and eye.

* *

FRONT

10" doll

THE RAPHAEL DRESS APRIL 1859 GODEY DIAGRAM PATTERN

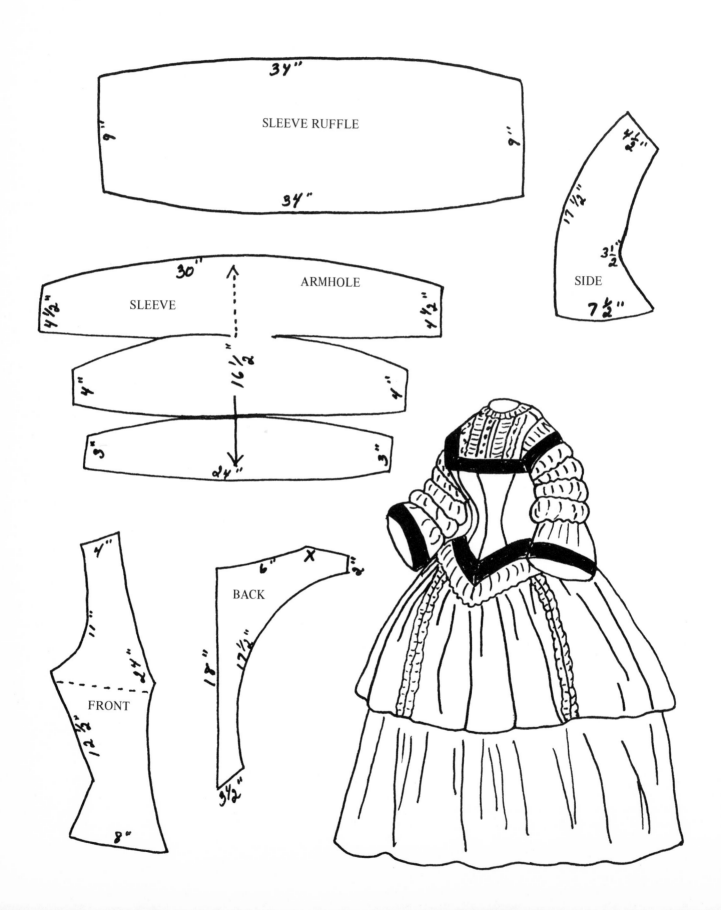

34"

SLEEVE RUFFLE

9"   9"

34"

4½"

17½"

3½"

SIDE

7½"

30"   ARMHOLE

4½"   SLEEVE   4½"

4"   4"

16½"

3"   3"

24"

4"

6"   X   2"

BACK

1"

4"

18"   17½"

FRONT

2½"

3½"

8"

VICTORIA PARDESSUS FEBRUARY 1859 GODEY

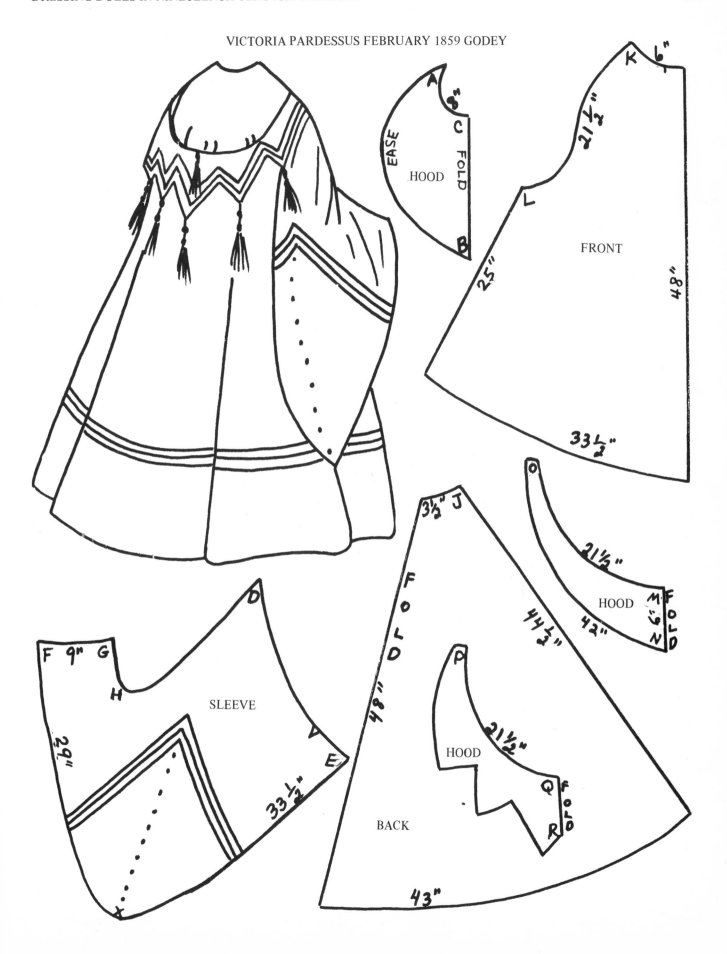

VICTORIA PARDESSUS FEBRUARY 1859 GODEY
(FITS 8" DOLLS)

It is distinguished for its style, combined with the ease and comfort with which it can be worn. The material is a gray speckled cloth, of which it can be made entirely. Although the French ladies have incorporated with it an amount of trimming that almost imparts to it the character of being composed of two materials. Thus, while the pardessus is chiefly framed of cloth, it has a border, and large portion of the hanging sleeve, in either black velvet or black moire antique. Rows of narrow black ribbon velvet also head these border trimmings.

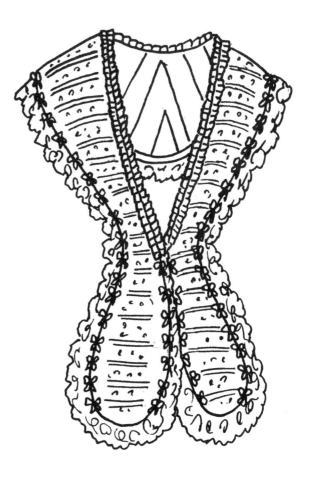

* * * * * * * * * * * * * * * * * * * *
AUTHOR'S NOTE:

MATERIALS: One-fourth yard fabric, one-fourth yard lining, small piece pelon interlining if desired, narrow cord or braid for trim, tiny buttons, snaps.

BODY

Cut material and lining, cut all pieces of hood on fold of material. Stitch cord or braid to sleeves. Sew sleeve D-E to back J down to V on sleeve. Sew D-H to K-L front piece. Sew side seams, then underarm seams of sleeves. Sew cord or braid trim to hemline as shown in drawing. Attach tiny buttons to the sleeves.

HOOD

Sew hood pieces 1 and 2 together at A-B and O-N, easing where necessary. Attach hood piece 3 matching O-M to P-Q. Trim hood with cord or braid as shown. Sew lining in the same manner. Close with snaps and sew tiny buttons on coat front or make real buttonholes. Make small tassels using heavy button thread or tatting thread and sew to each point or "vandyke" of hood as shown.

* * * * * * * * * * * * * * * * * * * *

MARIE ANTOINETTE FICHU JANUARY 1859 GODEY
(FITS 10" MANNIKIN DOLLS)

We have this month selected for illustration an article of dress which is at present in the highest fashion at Paris, and will, most probably, soon enjoy an equal degree of favor here. We speak of the Marie Antoinette Fichu. This elegant article has peculiar advantages. It can be worn with any dress, the plainer the better, and at once converts it into a dress costume; and is easily taken on and off.

The shape is first to be cut out in rather stiff net, over which puffings of thulle are to be laid at regular distances. Between each division either a narrow black ribbon or a pink satin ribbon is to be laid. The border is formed of a blonde about three inches wide, very slightly frilled. At the end of each of the ribbons which divide the puffings a bow is placed; from the part where the ends cross each other, these bows have their ends downwards. A quilling of ribbon is carried round the neck.

A plain bodice is given, which will make a plain dress, with a small sleeve added or may be sleeveless, with an under-sleeve made as shown in the sleeve section. Many bodices were made in this manner, and the sleeves were made separately, and attached to the particular bodice when worn.

* * * * * * * * * * * * * * * * * * * *
AUTHOR'S NOTE:

The fichu is very simple to make, and basically the directions are self-explanatory. All trimmings should be as narrow as possible. For small dolls, substitute a lace of three-fourths to an inch in width for the three-inch lace. A two-inch lace will do nicely for the larger size doll. For a very small doll use one-fourth inch ribbon folded in half lengthwise, giving the one-eighth inch width. This may also be used to make the tiny bows for the fichu fronts.

* * * * * * * * * * * * * * * * * * * *

MARIE ANTOINETTE FICHU JANUARY 1859 GODEY

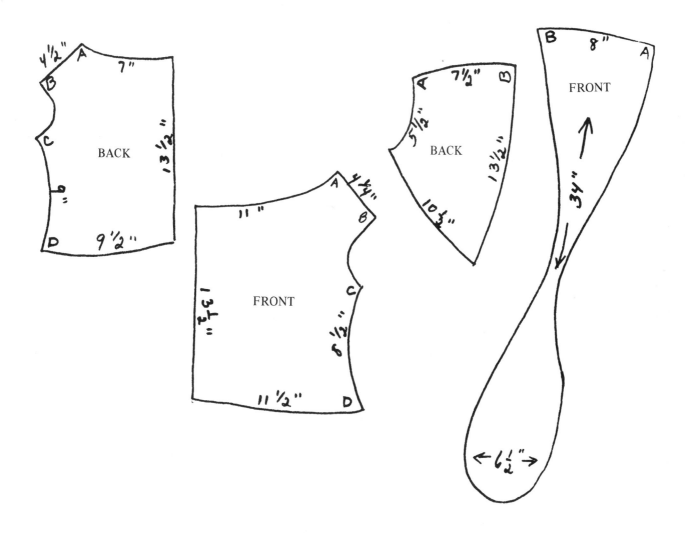

EMBROIDERY FOR CHEMISE BANDS

EMBROIDERY FOR CHEMISE YOKES

1859 Godey

THE ALMEDA.

1859 Godey

FALL DRESS.

1859 Godey

THE MARIONETTA.

1859 Godey

FOR THE MORNING CALL.

1859 Godey

LA MODE.

1859 Godey

THE COLSON.

1859 Godey

MORNING NEGLIGE.

1859 Godey

THE PICCOLOMONI ROBE DE CHAMBRE.

1859 Godey

SORTIE DU BAL.

[From the establishment of G. BRODIE, 51 Canal Street, New York.   Drawn by L. T. VOIGT, from actual articles
of costume.]

WE this month present a *sortie du bal*, or opera cloak, for the gay portion of our friends.   It is drawn from one made
of scarlet merino, with facings and vandykes of white taffeta upon the hood, front, the under portion of each sleeve, and
lower part of the cloak.   These are lozenged by lines of crimson chenille, each crossing being marked by a black spot of
the same.   Double rows of black and white lace edge the silk.   The sleeves are a marked novelty in construction.   Tassels
complete the garment.

1859 Godey

NEW STYLE GORED DRESS

1859 Godey

NEW STYLE GORED DRESS

1859 Godey

THE ZOUAVE JACKET.

1859 Godey

THE MOTHER.

1859 Godey

MORNING WRAPPER.

1859 Godey

AT HOME

1859 Godey

THE VISITING DRESS.

PART II

* * * * * * * * * * * * * * * * * * * *
AUTHOR'S NOTE:

THE 1860s

As we move into the 1860s we see a great change in fashions and accessories, as well as the introduction of some interesting new terms.

In this decade the dramatic Burnous cloak was very popular. Although it was worn in the 1850s, the design gained in popularity in the 1860s. Martha Johnson Patterson, daughter of President Andrew Johnson, wore this style cloak when she was White House Hostess. Her beautiful Burnous cloak is displayed at the Smithsonian Institution in the First Ladies Halls and is made of a material woven of white silk and goat's hair trimmed with gold scroll braid embroidery.

* * * * * * * * * * * * * * * * * * * *

JANUARY 1860 PETERSON

Among the new materials for the dresses of the present season we have observed some very rich silks, consisting of moires, striped and figured with bouquets, or with single flowers. Plain silk is becoming decidedly fashionable for dresses, and it is now worn in almost every tint. Of figured silks there are a great number in very pretty patterns. Plain and checquered satins and poplins have also appeared in great variety.

Front trimmings for the skirts of dresses continue in vogue. This style of ornamenting dresses forms a variety to the mode at present so popular, of trimming them with flounces.

Dresses for home and promenade are made high, closing in the front; the bodies fitting tight have the waists round, or but slightly pointed; bows or knots of velvet are worn down the centre, that at the waist terminating in long flowing ends. For dresses that have no flounces or second skirt, papillon or butterfly bows are very fashionable, they are placed entirely down the front of the dress. The small pointed pelerine or cape is in favor, or the body trimmed with a frill to imitate one, some ladies perferring the latter mode.

Sleeves are of various shapes. Some consist entirely of puffings reaching from the shoulder to the wrist. Others have small puffings above, and the lower part formed of one deep frill. Pagoda sleeves, or those narrow at top and wide at lower part, are among the favorites. Sleeves are sometimes made nearly close to the arm, and are finished at the end by a mousequetaire cuff. Those consisting of several frills, one above the other, are among the prettiest.

Among the prettiest dresses lately made, there is a dress of plain black silk which has just been completed. The skirt is trimmed with two deep flounces, each with two narrow gauffered frills. The corsage, high and buttoned up the front, is ornamented with a berthe pointed before and behind, and trimmed with two very narrow gauffered frills. The sleeves are wide pagodas, cut on the bias, they are finished at the lower edge with a double gauffered frill, and at the shoulder there is a gauffered trimming in the form of an epaulet. A ceinture of ribbon with a buckle is worn round the waist.

Bonnets for this season are rather larger than those worn during the past summer. They also sit closer round the face, and the brim advances somewhat more over the forehead than heretofore. Several have round crowns. They are composed of various materials, and the trimmings consist of feathers, velvet, blonde, lace, and ribbon. We have seen a bonnet of black velvet having the edge bordered with a row of red velvet; the curtain formed of black velvet, is edged with red. On the left side of the bonnet there is a cock's plume in red and black. Another bonnet composed of white silk, has been trimmed with brown ostrich feather. The curtain is composed of brown silk, and the strings of brown ribbon.

Cloaks are made full and rather-long, and several have wide hanging sleeves. Some have hoods, and others are covered at the upper part with a pointed pelerine, or with a square collar. One which is likely to be much in favor, is composed of gray cloth, and has wide flowing sleeves. It is pointed behind, and the point reaches to within a short distance of the edge of the dress. A small pointed pelerine of fichu covers the upper part, and the trimming consists of passementerie. Another cloak is in the form of a shawl, and is composed of black velvet ornamented with embroidery. It is trimmed with three deep flounces of black lace. Another black velvet cloak has a fichu-pelerine ornamented with embroidery and a trimming of fringe.

Jackets or Deep Basques are also exceedingly fashionable; they are equally divided in public favor with the cloaks. They are made of black, gray, or striped cloth, and are large and ample, having a peculiarity in the sleeve, which is cut extremely wide, and put in large plaits into the armhole, from whence it falls quite unconfined. This jacket has also a small collar and pockets.

HEAD DRESSES: The prettiest novelty for the season in the way of ornament for the hair, is a circlet of medallions, worn across the forehead. These are sometimes in cameos, sometimes in coral, and sometimes gilt coins laid on a band of black velvet. We have seen some gilt butterflies on a bandeau of black velvet, and scattered over the bows of black velvet behind the head, which had a very tasteful and fanciful effect.

* * * * * * * * * * * * * * * * * * * *
AUTHOR'S NOTE:

Department stores carry small cameo earrings; I have also seen some small coins on bracelets. These items of jewelry, taken apart, may be used to make the head dresses mentioned above.

* * * * * * * * * * * * * * * * * * * *

HOW-TO

Ladies in the country may like to have a simple cap suggested to them, which they can easily have made. Fold a piece of black net to about an inch wide, and let it be just long enough to reach to the sides of the face. Cut two little lappets about three inches long, and round at one end; tuck into them a very slight wire, and sew them on to the end of the foundation band. Attach a round crown. Fold a piece of net, and set it on as a curtain behind. This forms the foundation cap, which is to be trimmed with bows of ribbon at each side, placed on the lappets, and with bows and ends behind. Over this lay a row of white Maltese lace, plain in front, and fulled round the ears and behind; and over this is a diamond of black lace, or one crossed with ribbon velvet, finished round with a narrow black edging. In this way one of the prettiest caps of the season will be produced.

JANUARY 1860 PETERSON
EVENING DRESS OF WHITE TULLE

Evening Dress of white tulle, trimmed with eleven narrow tulle flounces, edged with blonde and narrow currant-colored velvet. A tunic of spotted tulle is trimmed with a broader velvet, a long wreath of velvet flowers, and a large bow of velvet ribbon. The sleeves and the berthe, which is of a heart-shape, are trimmed to correspond with the skirt. Wreath of green leaves and velvet flowers.

HEAD WEAR

Cap of white lace, with a deep curtain trimmed with lace. It is ornamented with two large rosettes of blue ribbon, and long, blue strings.

Head Dress of black velvet, composed of loops, bows, and ends.

PATTERN FOR BRAIDING

FEBRUARY 1860 PETERSON

Dresses are trimmed in various ways. When flounces are employed, there are several modes of arranging them, all equally fashionable. For instance, for dinner or evening dress the skirt may be entirely covered with narrow flounces; or they may be placed in groups of three and three together, reaching to a little above the knees. For a plainer style of dress, a favorite style for flounces consists of one deep flounce with a heading surmounted by three or four narrow frills, the uppermost having a heading. Flounces may be finished at the edge merely with a hem, or a row of velvet; or they may be pinked out in scallops. Trimmings composed of bands of velvet passing round the skirt, and front trimmings of velvet or passementerie, are also in vogue. In addition to those already mentioned, there are many favorite trimmings, consisting of gaufferings, macaroons, brandenbourgs, etc. Dresses are made quite high; the most in favor will be those with round waists and ceintures with broad floating ends; some ladies still prefer the pointed body, but in this case the points should be short, and the dresses lace up the back. Bows and rosettes down the front, in the whole length of the dress, have a very good effect, but this is only where the materials are heavy, and admit of neither flounces nor double skirts, or where there is no seam at the waist. Bows and ends in the form of shoulder knots are also popular. For indoor, the Zouave jacket, made of velvet, is worn with a skirt or satin; the skirts still continue to be worn as full as ever.

The Tight Sleeve will be the most stylish and fashionable, for morning and promenade dresses during the present season; it is a revival, with a few modifications, of the style of 1848, and is admirably adapted for those distingue dresses without seam across the waist. These sleeves are not made so very tight to the arm, as at the period above named; they have certainly a seam at the back of the arm to shape the elbow, but ample room is given to bend the arm easily; for cold weather they are decidedly more warm and comfortable than the large open sleeves, which have been carried to the extreme.

One of the prettiest dresses of the present season is composed of black velvet. It is made high and with the corsage closed up to the throat. With this exception of a row of gold buttons up the front of the skirt and the corsage, this dress is entirely plain. The sleeves are wide and lined with white satin, at the edge there is a row of white blonde covered with black lace. A ceinture of black velvet fastened with a gold buckle, is worn round the waist.

* *

AUTHOR'S NOTE:

The Rosetta diagram pattern would adapt well to the above style of dress.

* *

For Ball Dresses, tulle, tarletane, gauze, and very fine muslin, are the materials the best adapted; puffings of tulle always look light and elegant; the mixture of ribbon with the flowers is in very good taste, and will be in great favor; the ends of the ribbon always terminating either in gold acorns or tassels. A Paris paper describes a dress recently made for a Russian Princess, which must be very beautiful. The underslip was of white satin, over this was a skirt of tulle bouillonne, which was covered with a shower of golden stars; the corsage of the same. The dressmaker declared that the head dress was composed of five stars set in diamonds; a large one in the centre, and diminishing in size at the sides! Imagine the effect of this toilet on a young and beautiful creature, that creature possessing the additional lustre of being a princess, and this her toilet for the first ball after her marriage.

Another destined for the same person was composed of tulle of a pale delicate water-green, the skirt made with large bouillonnes, and looped up at irregular distances with branches of graceful hanging seaweed—this was called very appropriately the "Naiad".

* *

AUTHOR'S NOTE:

The two above dresses would make up beautifully for a doll's trousseau or for fairytale dolls such as Cinderella and Sleeping Beauty. The small gold spangled stars would serve nicely for the first dress described.

* *

Gold braid is being extensively introduced into ladies apparel this year; it first began with the Zouave jacket, and is now invading cloaks, dresses, and even bonnets; for cloaks it is not pretty—in the first place it tarnishes quickly, and in the second it has a stagey theatrical look, which every lady with quiet tastes wishes to avoid. For dresses the same remark may be made. For the Zouave, the little house jacket for cold weather, is lively, new, and coquettish.

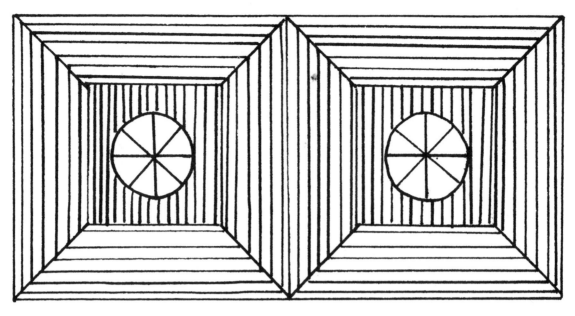

MACAROON PATCHWORK IN SILK AND VELVET

For morning and visiting collars, the fashionable stores are making us small all-rounders, in exact imitation of those worn by the gentlemen; they are very becoming. The sleeve to be worn with this is exactly like a gentlemen's shirt-sleeve, the cuff falling over the hand, and not turned back in the usual style. Both sleeves and collars are made of linen. Another pretty style is the col a revers. To use this shape the dress must be cut open in the front; the collar has lappets, which turn over leaving the neck slightly exposed. To avoid taking cold while adopting this pretty collar, the ladies tie about their necks a cravat, made of white muslin and trimmed with a deep Valenciennes. The bow and ends fit in exactly where the collar is open, and the effect is light and becoming. We must mention that with the first collar must be worn a cravat like those of the gentlemen, called in London, the "tubular tie".

Under-sleeves are worn a little fuller than recently. When not intended for evening dress they are closed at the wrists. Some are embroidered and trimmed with Valenciennes; others are trimmed with black lace, and bows and ends of velvet or ribbon are frequently employed as trimmings for under-sleeves. Fichus over low corsages are worn this winter.

Bonnets are much larger, coming more forward in the front, sitting off at the sides; terry velvet, mixed with lace and silk, is the fashionable material.

* * * * * * * * * * * * * * * * * * *
AUTHOR'S NOTE:

Terry velvet is available in our fabric stores. This gives us a good opportunity to buy this lovely material, in many different shades, to have on hand, when we are ready to make bonnets for our dolls.

* * * * * * * * * * * * * * * * * * *

1860 PETERSON
MACAROON PATCHWORK IN SILK AND VELVET

This is a new and beautiful pattern, for a species of work that is economical as well as fashionable; for it enables the fair worker to use up odd bits of velvet and silk that otherwise would be lost.

It is called the Macaroon Patchwork. It is made of two shapes, independently of the round of velvet from which it receives its title. The arrangement of color must depend upon individual taste, but the depth of shade must be carefully remembered. The interior square must be of a neutral tint, half of the side-pieces light, the other half dark, or black, which last has a very good effect.

The round, or macaroon of velvet, must be laid upon the central square of silk before it is tacked on to its paper shape, which is done by passing the needle through the centre, and making a long overcast-stitch, which reaches to the outer-rim, repeating this so as to form as many divisions as appear in our illustration. This is to be done in deep maize-color, or scarlet silk.

This patchwork of course, may be made of any size, by sewing together as many squares as are necessary, a border may be made large or small.

FEBRUARY 1860 PETERSON
BLACK SATIN DRESS

Dress of black satin trimmed with a fawn-colored satin plaided with black. The satin trimming is put on in scallops, around the bottom of the skirt are eight ruffles of the light satin, en tablier, and finished at the ends with black velvet bows. Body and sleeves trimmed to correspond with the skirt.

BLACK SATIN DRESS

MARCH 1860 PETERSON

Almost all the walking dresses are made with plain skirts, trimmed en tablier, or fastened up the front. A new way of setting in skirts at the waist, is to make four large flat plaits — one under each arm, and two behind.

Gimp trimmings for dresses and cloaks still hold their ground. Aiquilettes, buttons, bows, and with square ends, acorns trimmed with lace and enlivened with black beads, and flat graduated ornaments, both for bodies and skirts are all in demand.

Low corsages, worn with pelerines or fichus, are very fashionable for demi-toilet. The most favorite form for these fichus nearly resembles that of a half handerchief; that is to say, pointed at the back, and crossed over the bosom, the ends descending only to the waist, or hanging lower, according to taste. They are usually made on a foundation of white or black tulle, and are ornamented with rows of lace, with intervening runnings of ribbon or narrow rows of colored velvet. Rows of black and white lace, disposed alternately, are very

fashionable. The under-sleeves should correspond with the style of the fichu or pelerine with which they are worn. Those confined at the wrist frequently consist of several puffs, instead of one only, as heretofore; and between the puffs there are runnings of colored ribbon, with bows and flowing ends. Open sleeves are exclusively reserved for evening dress. They are equally trimmed in the manner of the fichus above described, with rows of lace, and intervening rows of narrow velvet. The velvet is frequently set on a lozenge pattern, and sometimes in small bows.

For morning dresses, small linen collars and cuffs, edged sometimes with colors, are worn, though white embroidery is more elegant. Thin muslin sleeves, with frills trimmed with guipure, are very pretty for demi-toilet. Some muslin sleeves have mousequetaire cuffs, lined with colored silk. These are trimmed round with a narrow Valenciennes, fluted. Collar to match.

The Zouave bodies, made of plain spotted muslin, are surrounded by puffing containing a ribbon, which is also run in the revers and round the short skirt behind.

The little showily trimmed aprons, formerly in such high favor for indoor morning dress, are again fashionable. This fashion is at once graceful and convenient. The silk dresses worn in outdoor costume are almost invariably plain in the skirts; or, if trimmed, they have tablier fronts.

Evening Dresses are generally cut straight, both in front and behind. They are usually finished at the top by a band of bouillonne, and trimmed with blonde or Valenciennes. The trimmings for corsages are, this season, very similar to those worn for some time past.

There is a new caprice in gloves, which has the merit of novelty, if not of beauty—none other than the long Spanish gloves, embroidered in gold and silver, and which will soon they say, become indispensable additions to a grand toilet.

1860 PETERSON
LADIES EMBROIDERED CRAVAT
AND DIAGRAM PATTERN

MATERIALS: Half yard colored silk, one skein embroidery silk.

In the design given may be found the proper shape and size cravat, observing to carry out the length of the ends, that they may measure 15 inches each, or else there will not be sufficient length to tie. Embroider as designed, then hold the silk under as marked by the lines B. A is the half of the piece to fit under the collar, and to which the ends are sewed. It is best to line the collar piece with bobbinet lace (net). The cravat may be made of any color plain silk. Embroider either with the same color, or with a shade darker, or with black. These cravats are at this time very fashionable and popular.

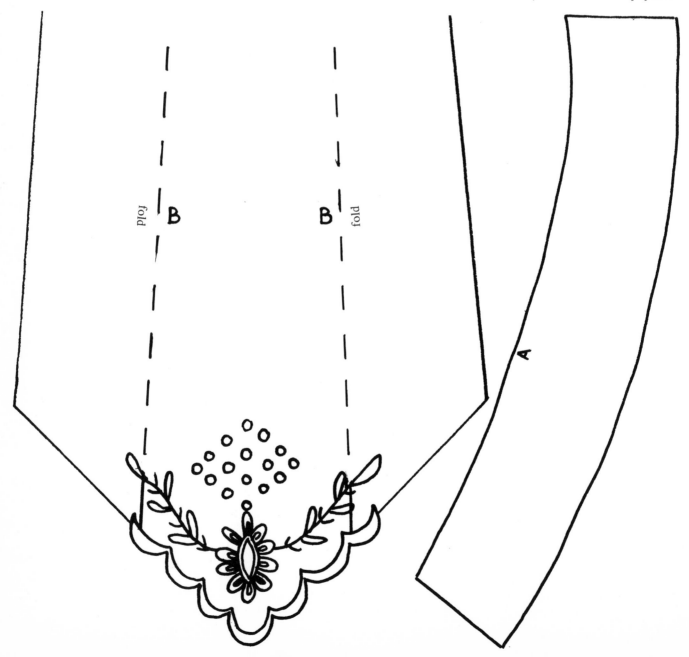

1860 PETERSON

FICHU OR CAPE

Marie Antoinette Cape of white blonde, trimmed with white and black lace, and on the shoulders and the back with narrow black velvet. The blonde is laid in deep plaits from the shoulders.

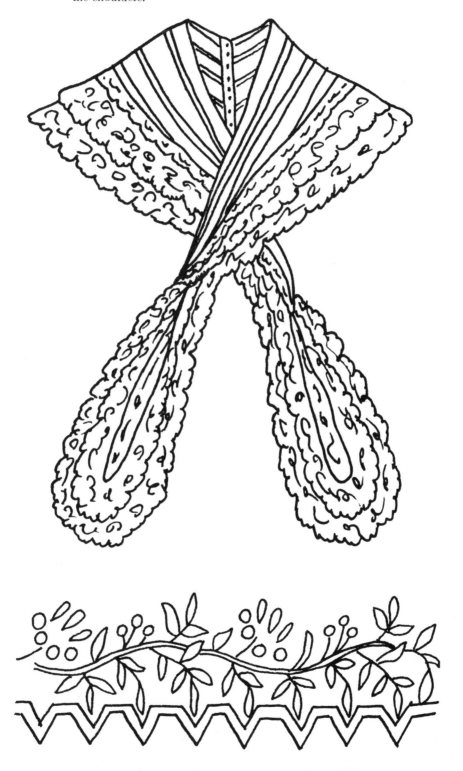

FOR BOTTOM OF PETTICOAT

MARCH 1860 PETERSON

NEW STYLE BODY

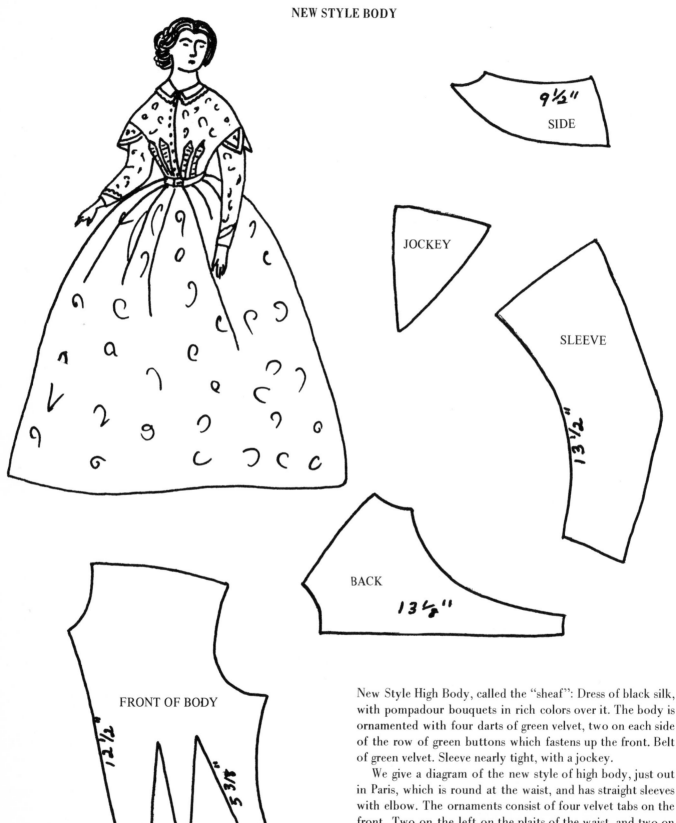

New Style High Body, called the "sheaf": Dress of black silk, with pompadour bouquets in rich colors over it. The body is ornamented with four darts of green velvet, two on each side of the row of green buttons which fastens up the front. Belt of green velvet. Sleeve nearly tight, with a jockey.

We give a diagram of the new style of high body, just out in Paris, which is round at the waist, and has straight sleeves with elbow. The ornaments consist of four velvet tabs on the front. Two on the left on the plaits of the waist, and two on the right; also of three similar tabs placed one in the middle at the bottom of the back, and one on each of the side seams. These tabs are narrow at bottom, and lance-shaped at top.

APRIL 1860 PETERSON

The few new Spring goods which have yet appeared are very beautiful. The most expensive silks have solid colored grounds, with small flowers embroidered over them. Small checks and pin stripes are also very fashionable, and much less expensive than the embroidered silks. These latter are to be made with plain skirts, while the checks and pin-stripes will be most generally ruffled. The colors are exquisite in many of the new silks; the shades of green, lilac, and mode colors, are prettier than ever before. Foulard silks are generally in chintz patterns, on black ground; and the same may be said of delaines, except that the grounds are of light colors. Grenadines are of every style, though those with many small flounces or ruffles will be the most popular. Organdies and lawns will be generally ruffled, and some have as many as fifteen ruffles, though seven, nine, or eleven are the usual number. A ball dress lately made of white tarletane had as many as twenty-five ruffles. The handsomest, but also the most expensive walking dresses now worn, are certainly those which are embroidered with the hand on the corsage and in front of the skirt. This is very fashionable and very rich; the work is generally the same color as the dress, and the effect is really beautiful.

There is some variety in the manner of trimming dresses. A dress of black silk has a trimming of six flounces, each edged with blue silk. The flounces are arranged three by three, a puffing which surmounts of the first three, separating them from the rest. The corsage of this dress is trimmed with small quillings of blue silk; it is not pointed at the waist, and a belt is worn with it. The sleeves are formed at the upper part of two puffs, above which a bow of ribbon is disposed as an epaulet; at the lower part the sleeves are shaped to the elbow.

The travelling dresses, walking dresses, or other dresses made of heavy material like pique or Marseilles, those without seams at the waist are getting more in favor. These robes must have a seam in front from the manner in which they are cut, so must necessarily be trimmed down the front with buttons, bows of ribbon or rosettes.

The Compiegne, or Isabeau, as it is sometimes called will with some be a favorite style of walking dress, the body crossing from the right side to the left, not closing to the throat, but having small lapels turned back; the skirt opening at the sides taking the same slanting direction as the body. These dresses are sometimes buttoned down, or are fastened by means of narrow straps and small buckles.

Tight sleeves will not be so popular as the warm weather advances, and the extremely large ones will be generally used, except for travelling dresses. The predictions with regard to crinoline being abolished, seem not to have been fulfilled, for the Empress of the French still wears hers expanded to nearly its usual extent, and as she rules the French ladies most despotically in the matter of fashion, and as the French ladies rule us, we suppose that crinoline will still hold its own, though we hope with diminished size. Some courageous ladies made their appearance at the Tuileries lately without hoops, but the change was almost too violent. If the hoops could be reasonably reduced in size, the appearance of the ladies would be improved, and their health would not suffer, as it will most certainly do, when hoops are entirely abolished.

Mantillas are cut so as to fall over the arm in the old pelerine fashion, with long, square tabs in front.

Head Dresses of gold and silver plaits with pendant tassels, intermingled with the hair, from very elegant head-dresses. One of the newest head dresses in the style called petit-bord, is composed of red velvet and gold net. On one side, a long, white ostrich feather waves over the shoulder, and on the opposite side a lappet of black lace, fixed by an ornament formed of loops of gold braid.

Fans, ornamented with spangles of steel and gold, continue to be fashionable. The material usually employed for mounting these fans are tulle and crape, either colored or white.

THE COMPIEGNE

The corsage of this wraps over and fastens on the left side. The skirt is very wide at the lower part, and is trimmed with a band of velvet, edged with gold. Square pocket-holes trimmed with velvet and gold. Long sleeves, set in full at the armholes, and trimmed down the outside of the arm with bands of gold. The cuffs are trimmed in corresponding style, and fastened with buttons of velvet and gold. Round the throat a narrow ruff of quilled tulle, and cuffs of the same. Of course any colored braid may be substituted for the gold braid.

(See next page for illustration.)

MAY 1860 PETERSON

Gray silks seem to be the favorite for out-of-door wear this spring, or a minute plaid of black and white, which has the effect of gray. One of our fashionable dressmakers had thirty-five gray silks at one time in the house to be made up. This color is always quiet and lady-like, so will always be popular. Still for those who fancy brighter hues, there are the various shades of lilacs, blues, and greens, of most exquisite tints. The lawns and organdies that are not flounced are mostly in stripes with large figures. Grenadines and bareges, on the contrary, if not flounced have rather small figures.

Small ruffles or flounces are very much in favor, though some have only four or five narrow ruffles at the bottom of the skirt. A few dresses have double skirts, the lower one being ruffled, and the upper skirt reaching to the top ruffle.

Sleeves continue to be made quite large, with but little trimming, especially in silk dresses.

The Robe Imperatrice, or Polonaise, as it is now sometimes called, is very popular with our fashionable dressmakers. The body and skirt of this dress are cut in one piece, like a very deep basque. For those who may like a quieter style, bodies with sharp points behind and in front are being made. Although, as a general thing, all skirts are put on in very large, hollow plaits; still some few of the new dresses have the skirts gathered on around the points, quite in the old style.

Gored skirts are almost entirely worn. This kind of skirt is very graceful, as it throws the fulness to the back, and prevents the great bunches on the hips, which a very full skirt necessarily has. A gored skirt is usually four and a half to five yards wide at the bottom, and about three yards at the top. The new hoop skirts are made in a bell shape to suit the dresses cut in this style.

MANTILLA FOR MAY

THE COMPIEGNE

(See previous page for description.)

1860 PETERSON
MANTILLA FOR MAY AND DIAGRAM

One of the prettiest mantillas, which we have seen this season, it has been drawn from one imported from Paris. The material is black silk.

We give a diagram, from which, when enlarged, the mantilla can be cut out. Any lady can make this mantilla.

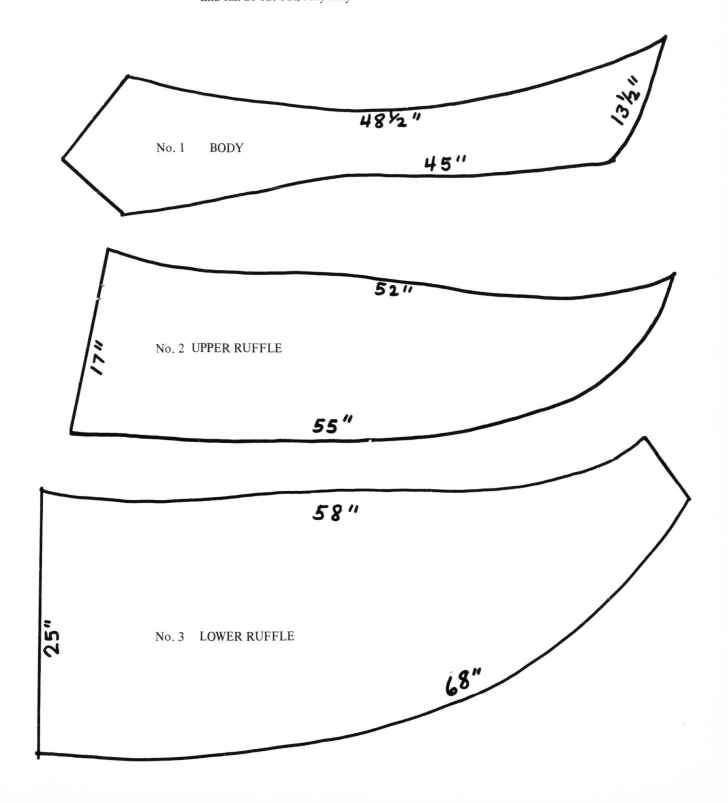

No. 1   BODY
48½"
13½"
45"

No. 2 UPPER RUFFLE
52"
17"
55"

No. 3   LOWER RUFFLE
58"
25"
68"

WHITE BODY AND SLEEVES

UNDER-SLEEVE

RAPHAEL CAPE

JUNE 1860 PETERSON

Small ruffles continue to be very much worn. Not only the small checked summer silks are trimmed with them, but bareges, grenadines, and organdies, are frequently ruffled. Nearly all thin dresses are made low in the neck, with pretty little capes; though for those who prefer high-necked dresses, many are cut half-high, as in the "LAWN DRESS WITH A DOUBLE SKIRT", or high at the back opening part way down to the waist. Round or pointed waists are both equally worn. Sleeves are made very wide.

Trimmings for dresses are various. The newest, and one of the most popular, being a kind of rosette, having a silk button of the color of the dress which it is to trim, in the centre, and a row of black around it. Then there is a flat, plaited cord, and various ribbon trimmings.

The new materials for travelling dresses are very beautiful being usually combinations of black and white, or a soft gray hue. The fabrics are usually composed of woolen and silk, or linen and silk, in various combinations. These materials and colors are equally popular for walking dresses, being quiet in tone and reasonable in price. For either travelling or walking dresses, the mantillas, or sacque, is made of the same material as the dress. But little trimming is allowed. It should be with a galloon or a flat plaited cord corresponding with the dress. Nothing is neater than one of these dresses with a plain linen collar and sleeves, which are sufficiently cheap and easily ironed to be frequently changed, and can, therefore, be kept immaculate in their whiteness. In fact, linen collars and sleeves have entirely superseded the fine embroidered muslin ones for the street.

Mantillas are various in their styles. The lace ones are of the scarf shape, coming off the shoulders, but those of silk are nearly all high in the neck. For young ladies very deep basques or casques, are the most popular; they reach to within half of the bottom of the dress. Those which are not made in this way, have very full, deep ruffles or skirts, plaited on to a pointed yoke or body, which reaches nearly to the waist behind.

Bonnets of very coarse straw, trimmed with black ribbons figured with straw-color, are popular. A bunch of wheat-ears, or a cluster of oats, is frequently added to these bonnets, making the effect at once simple and elegant. Capes are small, and but little trimmings is allowable on a coarse straw bonnet.

JUNE 1860 PETERSON
SCARF MANTELET,
STANDING COLLAR, AND SLEEVE

White Muslin Scarf Mantelet. This is one of the prettiest novelties of the season. There is a deep embroidered ruffle around the scarf, which is headed by a plaiting of muslin.

Standing Collar And Sleeve in batiste, of the form called the Col Chevaliere. It is intended to be worn with the sleeve, and is attached to a habit-shirt of Swiss Muslin, with folds or tucks in front.

SCARF MANTELET

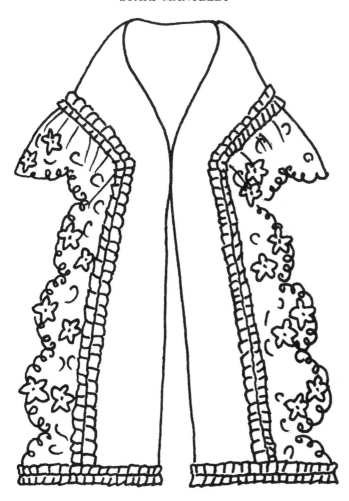

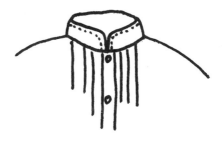

STANDING COLLAR

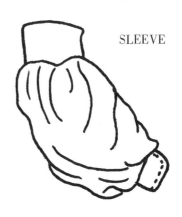

SLEEVE

JULY 1860 PETERSON

Dresses for the promenade have the skirts very wide at the bottom, slightly gored toward the waist, and are considered very stylish without flounces, but the lighter materials, such as taffetas, thin glaces, and all of that class will have flounces still, and even a second skirt to meet the flounces.

Bodies are made high for out-of-door costume, closing in front with small buttons, the waists round with belts or waistbands of ribbon; a very pretty belt is being introduced; it is of narrow gilt leather, and fastens by a small gold buckle; it is quite a novelty, and looks extremely well on silk or poplin dresses.

Sleeves for the warm weather are made quite open and large; the close sleeve being almost totally abandoned at present. Muslin chemisettes and sleeves with Swiss plaits are much worn with low-bodied dresses, especially by young ladies. Fichus and pelerines of tulle, muslin, or lace, are also again in favor. They cross on the breast, and terminate in wide, rounded ends, or in pointed ends which fasten under the sash. Among the head dresses lately imported, there is one consisting of a bandeau of black and violet powdered with gold stars, and accompanied by two tufts, one very compact, of silk violets,

and the other of black and violet velvet bows mixed with gold threads, to match the velvet bandeau. Another is a torsade of wide mallow-ribbon blended with black lace, and fastened at the side by an agrafe of wheat-ears in silver.

1860 PETERSON

THE ROSETTA

DESCRIPTION AND INSTRUCTIONS:

This is a very fashionable dress, just out in Paris. The sleeve, it will be seen, is cut so as to form a very wide pagoda bottom. There is no plait at top, and the pattern is all of one piece, which makes both the sleeve and revers. About the straight part of the stuff several plaits are made so as to raise that part the distance required to meet the seam in front of the sleeve, which is hollowed out at the bend, to give it the appearance of a wide sleeve with an elbow. The inner side of this sleeve would round off at bottom, and be wider than the outer part, so as to leave visable the ruche put inside.

This sleeve is ornamented with a plain revers formed out of the same pattern, which is folded back in front, above the seam at the bend of the arm. This revers, beginning in front of the sleeve-hole, covers the seam, the beginning of the plaits, and joins the bottom of the sleeve at the corresponding mark, a star. This revers is bordered by a narrow lace gathered very full, and has three buttons on it encircled by two rows of narrow lace very full; a fourth button similarly surrounded seems to fasten the beginning of the revers at the bottom of the sleeve behind.

The body of this dress has no seam at the waist; a side-piece is put in front to join the letters A and B. The back of this body is composed of three parts; the first that forming the middle, meets a side-piece at the letters C and D; this first side-piece meets a second at the letters E and F. When these seams are made, the front and back of the body are complete, and are joined by the seam under the arm. When the seams of the body are sewed, the stuff that remains free at bottom, behind, and in front, is laid in the plaits round the waist.

The seams of the skirt should be made and cut sloping off toward the waist. The bottom of the skirt must be at least five yards round.

* *
AUTHOR'S NOTE:

When cutting pattern widen skirt to give shaping as seen in drawing. Make length of skirt to fit doll.

* *

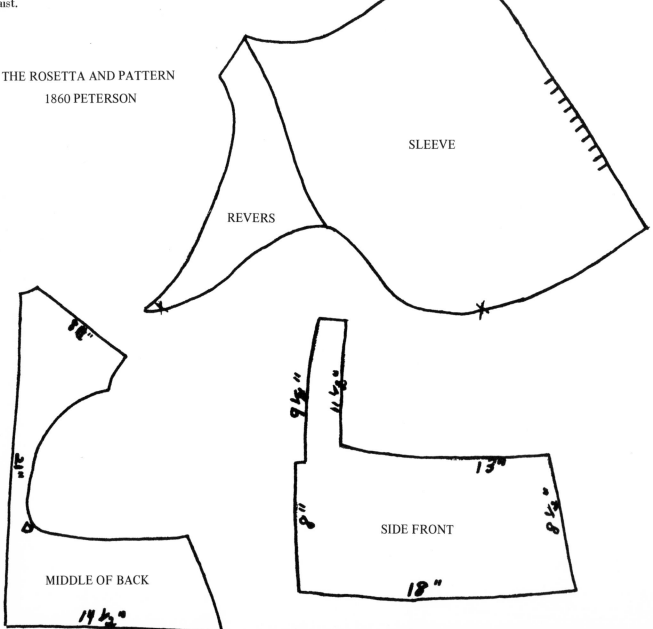

THE ROSETTA AND PATTERN

1860 PETERSON

SLEEVE

REVERS

MIDDLE OF BACK

14½"

SIDE FRONT

18"

9½"   11½"

8"   8½"

13"

THE ROSETTA AND PATTERN
1860 PETERSON

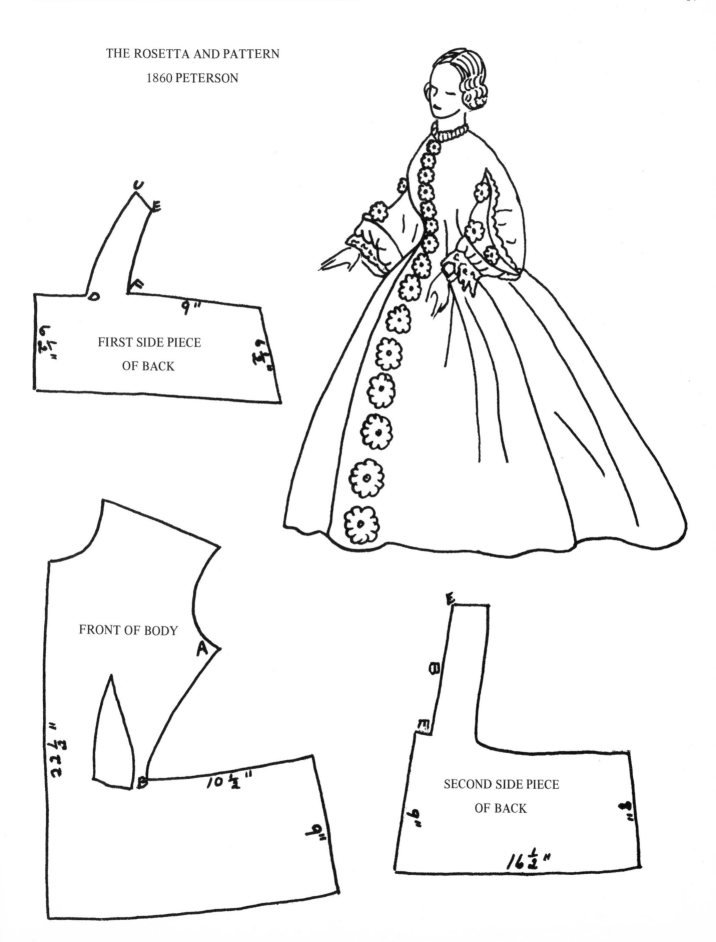

FIRST SIDE PIECE
OF BACK

FRONT OF BODY

SECOND SIDE PIECE
OF BACK

1860 PETERSON

TO CROCHET A SUN HAT

MATERIALS: Four balls crochet cord, gray or brown.

Make a chain of 6. Join and work in double crochet, widening enough to keep the work flat. Do a piece large enough for the crown, then make a chain long enough to fit around the crown. Join it and crochet 11 rows. After which do 13 rows for the rim, widening gradually. Finish with 1 row shell work; crochet the crown piece and face together.

Take the hat to milliner to be stiffened and pressed; wire the edge, and line the hat either with plain lawn the same color, or with pink or blue. Trim with the lawn as wide as ribbon; hem on both sides, or pink the edges of the lawn, and make a full box quilling to go around the crown; bows and ends hemmed. Either a piece of elastic in piece of strings, or strings, as the fancy may suggest.

* *

AUTHOR'S NOTE:

Follow directions above, but use a size 20 crochet thread and a size 11 metal crochet hook, for a doll size hat.

* *

BORDER FOR PETTICOAT

AUGUST 1860 PETERSON

The two most fashionable colors are known by the titles of the Magenta and the Solferino. The first of these is an extremely agreeable and refreshing green, with a tinge of blue in its shade, the second a sort of intense, deep-toned, brilliant peach, inclining to what is understood by the dahlia color. It is not necessary to say that both of these have received their names in France. Gray, however, is the fashionable color for travelling dresses, or ordinary walking dresses. It has the advantage of not being conspicuous on the street, and of not showing dust. The material for these dresses is very varied, nearly all, however, having a little wool and silk in it, and ranging in price from twelve and a half cents, up to one dollar and a quarter. A very excellent and pretty dress may be bought from twelve and a half to twenty-five cents a yard.

Small Ruffles are still very much on nearly all kinds of dresses, but they do not generally extend much higher than the knee.

Zouave Jackets of black silk or cashmere, embroidered in either black, crimson, or gold, are very much worn over light summer dresses, as well as those of thin white muslin.

Ball Dresses are of extreme elegance; rich white satin trimmed in various ways, either with tulle and flowers, or rich lace flounces looped with bouquets are in favor. Light colored tulles and silk gauze are also much worn; emerald green, pink, and pale-blue, being the favorite colors; white tulle with gold or silver stars or spots has a charming effect; the bodies have the waists round with broad sashes; the fronts crossed by draperies or folds, and the sleeves full.

Bonnets this season are extremely elegant; white chip mixed with crape, tulle, or blonde for dress bonnets; while for morning wear there is soft leghorn, and those fine straws which always have so fresh and charming an appearance for young ladies.

AUGUST 1860 PETERSON

ZOUAVE JACKET AND DIAGRAM PATTERN

We this month give a drawing and diagram of a new style of Zouave Jacket. The pattern consists of four pieces, the front, back, side-piece, and sleeve; we have given a different style of sleeve to that in the costume; it is fulled at the top instead of being plain, and may be lengthened as much as required; some ladies are wearing them the length of the pattern only: the sleeves of the chemisette should always be the very full bishop. The jacket may either be ornamented by arabesques, or braided round in any design, such as the Grecian border, etc. The front of chemisette is cut on the bias, so as to sit full over the top of the skirt. The jacket will be very much worn this autumn, made in cashmere, and braided with a contrasting color.

ZOUAVE JACKET AND DIAGRAM PATTERN

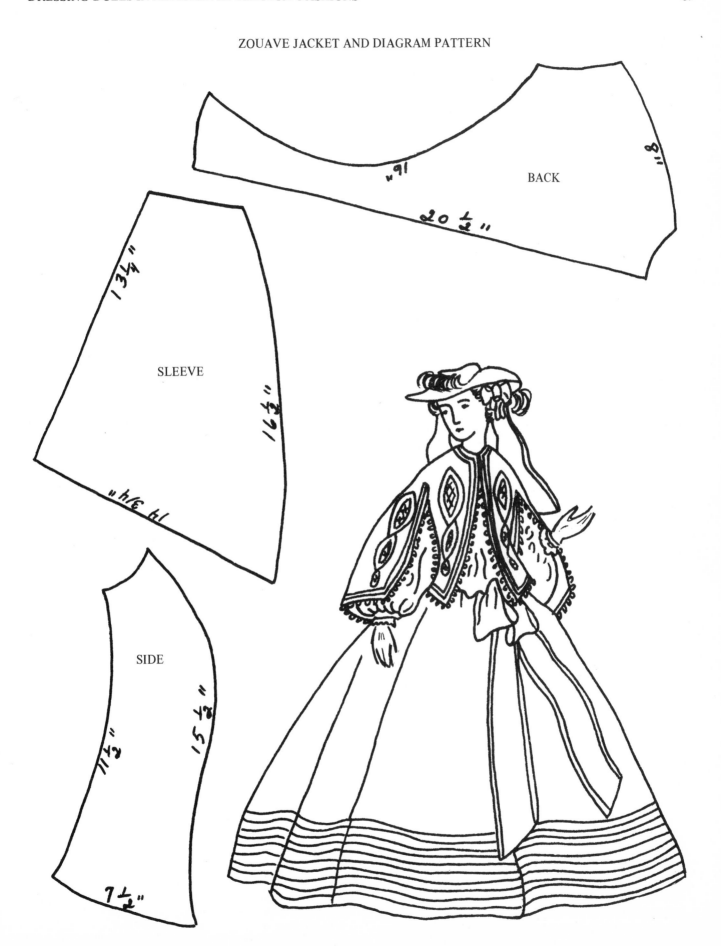

ZOUAVE JACKET AND DIAGRAM PATTERN
AUGUST 1860 PETERSON

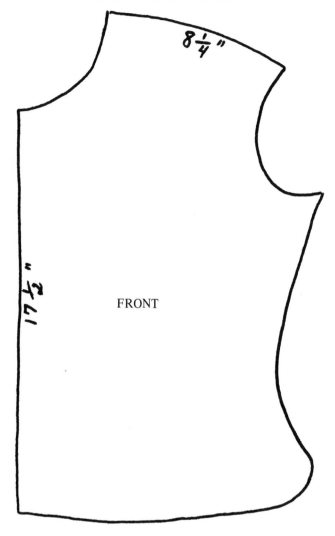

8¼"

17¼"

FRONT

SEPTEMBER 1860 PETERSON

Nearly all the new silk dresses are being made without a seam at the waist, trimmed down the front by rosettes of lace or passementerie. Some silk dresses are made open to the waist with lappels turned back; the sleeves tight, with large puffings at the top, and deep cuffs turned back. Other dresses have bodies plain, fastened by buttons, and trimmed all down the front by a series of bows or gimp ornaments; sleeves wide, lined with white and bordered just inside by a small white ruche; in some instances sleeves are slashed and the bodice pointed. Even where the skirt is set on to the body, it is almost invariably gored, in order to have but little fullness at top. Flounces are only worn around the lower part of the skirt.

Sleeves are still of the wide pagoda form, the pagoda, Isabeau, and Mandarin all being synonymous, and varying only in the degree of width given to them.

The combination of black and white in the toilet is still prevalent. One of the prettiest dresses at a wedding party lately, was composed of white tarletane figured with black spots.

The skirt was trimmed with three broad flounces, each headed by two narrow ones. All these flounces were edged with black lace. On one side of the skirt there were four bows of cherry-color velvet. The corsage had a berthe formed of three folds of tarletane, and was trimmed with black lace and bows of cherry velvet. The short sleeves were covered by pointed loose sleeves over them, and trimmed with black lace and cherry-colored velvet ribbon.

Casaques of black silk will be very much worn this fall. There are several varieties of this wrap, some closing in their entire length and fitting loose, but slightly defining the waist; others closing to the waist and fitting the figure perfectly; some fit in the waist at the back, but fall loose in the front like a mantle, the skirts of these casaques should descent to within about ten or twelve inches of the bottom of the dress: the sleeves are always large of the Isabeau form, either finished by quillings or plaitings, or have cuffs turned back or imitated by the trimming.

Paletots which fit close, or nearly close, to the figure, have generally a pelerine, which is small and pointed, and may be composed either of silk, trimmed with fringe, a plaiting of ribbon, or lace, or may be made entirely of guipure. In Paris, narrow straw trimmings are used to border either the hems of mantles and casaques; or where they are trimmed with frills or flounces, the edges are finished by a narrow band of straw. When straw is not liked, white silk is sometimes used, of a very narrow embroidery or two or three rows of narrow silk cord round these black silk mantles, are a very distingue trimming.

Bonnets are worn larger, more raised in the front, and still falling off at the sides. The mixture of black and white is in great favor. Field flowers are used in ornamenting straw bonnets. For white chip, tulle, and crape feathers, black and white lace, and flowers, are all equally fashionable. Plain straws or Leghorn, are sometimes tastefully trimmed with a black and white aigrette, bows of ribbon and flowers, peacocks or pheasants feathers, or a cock's plume. Ornaments of straw may also be mentioned among the fashionable trimmings for bonnets. These ornaments consist of twists, tassels, small, light, curled ornaments, called mouches, and pompons, which are sometimes placed within the puff of tulle or lace, and sometimes are intermingled with ribbon. Even the black, brown, and gray straws are trimmed with a small bouquet of red or blue corn flowers; the strings and curtain of the same hue as the bonnet. A very small veil of black lace is frequently adopted with these bonnets.

The New Collars, of linen or plain cambric muslin, are terminated in front by two embroidered ends crossing each other, and fastened together by a very large button of enameled gold, jasper or amethyst. The cuffs to match, which serve as wristbands to very voluminous puff-puff sleeves of muslin or tarletane, are also fastened at the side by a large button, beyond which there is a small embroidered like extremity of a waistband. (We give drawings of these in the present number).

Kid Gloves, or those of Saxon leather embroidered, may now, more easily than ever, be found to match the colors of the dress, for we see them of several new tints, such as gilly-flower, deep green, and blue; but very light gloves, as straw or maize, will always be the most stylish, and the only ones that form a suitable complement to an elegant toilet.

As we have before said, black and white are blended in all parts of the toilet. It is found even in walking shoes, which are black kid stitched with white silk. Boots of satin delaine, or of silk, to match the prevailing color of the toilet, are also in good wear; likewise kid boots with coutil gaiters and a rosette in front; or bronze kid with silk gaiters. To our taste, however, nothing is so elegant as a plain black, elegantly fitting gaiter, or black kid slipper and open worked stockings.

When buttons are worn on the dress, the tight-sleeve is slit up to a certain height, and buttoned behind the arm with large buttons like those on the front of the body. These buttons are continued down the front of the skirt in the cassock or Empress dresses, which are quite plain in front, and laid in wide plaits behind and at the sides.

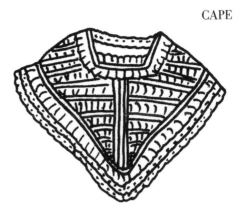

CAPE

CHEMISETTE

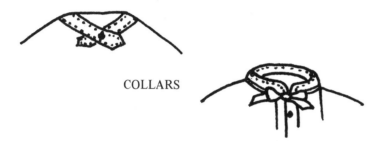

COLLARS

STRAW BONNET

CUFF

PLUMED BONNET

ACCESSORIES SEPTEMBER 1860 PETERSON

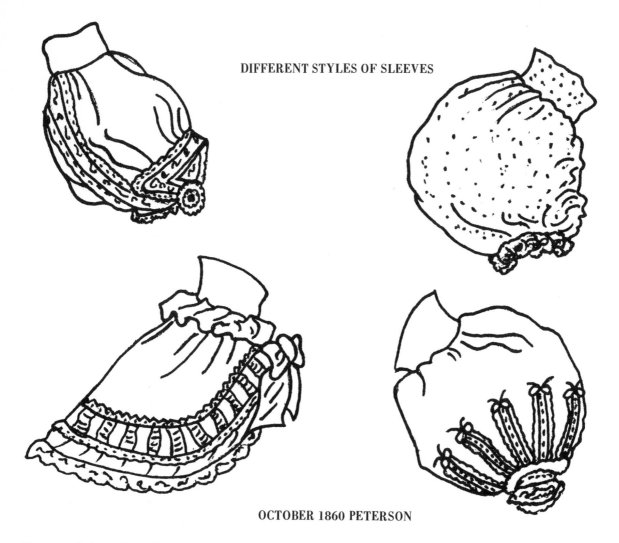

DIFFERENT STYLES OF SLEEVES

OCTOBER 1860 PETERSON

The most fashionable style of silks (in fact of all the new goods) is a black or some other dark ground, with quite small flowers in a single color, sprinkled over the ground. Thus black and gold, or black and crimson; dark blue and browns, green and gold; purple and black, are very elegant.

Narrow ruffles are still worn on silks of light textures, but the heavier kinds of goods will be made with plain skirts. Bows of ribbon, rosettes, and velvet will all be largely employed during the coming season for ornamenting dresses. Some prefer one deep flounce, headed by two or three quite narrow ones, or by a puffing to the narrow ruffles. But a great deal is left to the individual taste; ruffled skirts and plain skirts, close sleeves, and large, loose sleeves. Quaker-like plainness and a great deal of trimming; tight-fitting basques and exceedingly full mantles, are all equally fashionable. The mixture of black and white is more than ever in favor.

For instance, crape and white tulle bonnets, trimmed with bunches of black and white flowers or fruit; chemisettes and canzous plaited in the Swiss style, with black velvet revers or rolls, and even tarletane and muslin dresses covered with alternate black and white flounces; while similar flounces decorate sleeves and body. Velvet ribbon, about two inches wide, makes pretty trimming for the skirt of a dress, put on in vandykes

round the bottom of which it covers about five-eighths of a yard. At the point of each is a tied bow of the same velvet ribbon. Graduated bows up the front of the dress, with small steel buckles in the centre, sometimes take the place of the rosettes which are so much worn.

All skirts should be slightly gored (one breadth on each side is just enough to set them out well), and sloped two or two and a half inches at the bottom, from the front to the back, to prevent so much slope at the top. In mounting a skirt on to the body, the fullness should be arranged in five or six small pleats on each side of the front, and in three or four large box pleats behind. Sleeves of almost every shape are worn; a few of the tight ones, and some half-tight.

Large buttons, called macaroons, surrounded with lace, are in great favor as ornaments for redingotes or a simple style of dress.

Passementerie, which has so long played an important part in toilettes, will continue so to do; it is much employed both for robes and mantelets.

For dress trimmings, gimps in all the fancy styles are very much used. These gimps are also used on cloaks and other out-of-door wraps, in the shapes of medallions, loops, etc.

NOVEMBER 1860 PETERSON

CHEMISETTE FOR ZOUAVE

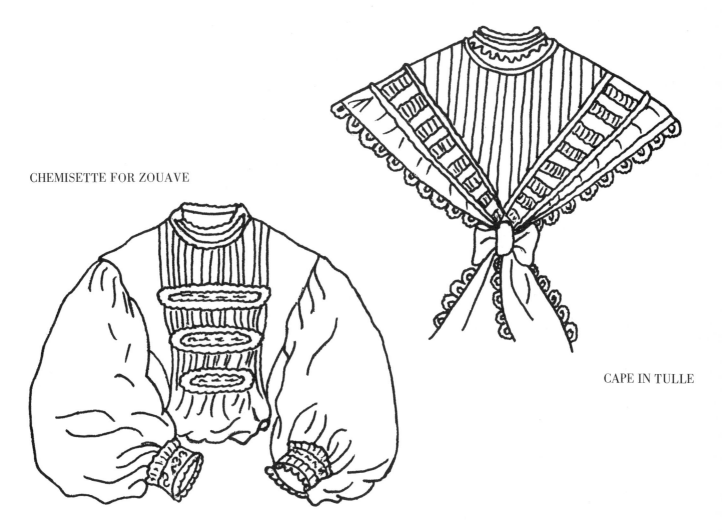

CAPE IN TULLE

NOVEMBER 1860 PETERSON

Several of the newest silk dresses are trimmed with flounces, and a pretty variety is obtained when the flounces are of two different colors. For example, flounces composed of the same silk as the dress, are often placed alternately with others of a tint harmonizing with them, or they may be formed of two different shades of the same color. We have seen a dress trimmed with lilac and violet flounces, and another with flounces in two tints of green. Sometimes the flounces are disposed in separate sets, or series, and with them are intermingled narrow pinked ruches. A bias row of silk of the darker shade is also placed on the edge of the skirt. The corsages of these dresses are high, and the sleeves either long or demi-long. The trimming on the corsages and sleeves should correspond with that on the skirt. Merinoes of plain colors will be much worn. Indeed these very serviceable dresses must always remain fashionable from necessity. Figured merinoes are also popular, as well as delaines of dark grounds with gay chintz-colored palms and flowers. In Paris, cloth dresses are extremely fashionable, and they are made in very elegant style. Some have the corsages richly embroidered with silk, others with braid. Many ladies who have adopted cloth dresses, have had them made with corsages opening with lappels, and showing a vest. This is in some sort the revival of a fashion which was very general a few years ago. The vest worn with a cloth dress should be of same material as that employed in lining and lappels of the corsage, which may be either silk or velvet. The vest, however, is not generally adopted. The skirts of these cloth dresses are invariably plain, and the sleeves may be either close at the wrists, with turn-up cuffs or demi-wide with revers. Heavy materials, such as cloth or velvet, are frequently made with a skirt and long casaque, fitting closely to the figure. For a cloth dress made in this style, a trimming of rich passementerie is very effective.

SLEEVE STYLES

DECEMBER 1860 PETERSON

Dresses for the house have the skirts long, extremely wide at the bottom, this width being reduced at the top by the breadths being gored; the fullness is set into the waist in large, hollow plaits; this refers equally to silks, poplins, mohairs and all the more substantial materials. For silk dresses, narrow flounces are fashionable, either trimmed with narrow black lace or the edges pinked. Deep fullings of silk divided into puffings by straps of narrow black velvet, is also a very stylish trimming. Fluting is also very much employed on the skirts, sleeves, and bodies of dresses. The extent to which it is used is quite remarkable, and its variety in width, in application, endless. This fluting is made by putting on a trimming of silk or velvet in deep box-plaits, which are caught at the bottom of and fastened by a stitch. This gives the fluted appearance to the trimming. In Paris there have been a good many silk dresses made in the following style: at the bottom of the skirt one broad flounce, cut the bias way, and surmounted by a narrow flounce forming a heading to the broad one. Both flounces are cut out at the edges, and a second jupe, finished with a hem, descends just to the top of the narrow flounce. A broad ceinture of silk the same as the dress, and with fringed ends, is fastened on one side of the waist, the ends flowing over the skirt. Another favorite style of trimming for silk dresses consists of a broad band of velvet, the color of the silk placed quite at the edge of the skirt.

Flounces will be the ornament mostly used on silk dresses; either several narrow ones to the knee, or one larger surmounted by narrower ones, or by a trimming.

Bodies of dresses are made high and generally closed to the throat, though those made slightly opened in front are becoming more popular; these last have pieces like the lappels of a coat turned back; sometimes these lappels or revers are of the same material as the dress, and sometimes of velvet. Waists of nearly all dresses, except evening dresses are made round, and have narrow belts and clasps, or a sash of the same material as the dress. Wide, open sleeves are still worn, but they are narrower at the top than the sleeves of last winter. Some tight sleeves have also made their appearance again; but for close sleeves, those puffed from the shoulder to the waist are preferred, though some have been made tight to the elbow, with three puffings above.

Nets are still worn both in neglige and full dress. Some have every mesh covered by a little gold star, others are entirely of gold with a small coronet of pompons forming a bandeau, and others again are made of large cords of silk. A beautiful net made lately to wear with a white dress trimmed with daisies, had the meshes composed of very small daisies.

Paletots or loose sacques, made long, with a collar and wide sleeves, are considered the most fashionable. Some are made in a mixture of cotton and wool, and with pockets, have a smart appearance. Gray, trimmed with ribbon, and with large buttons of the same color, is a favorite. Those in black silks are more dressy. They are either plain or finished with a guipure passementerie, or a quilling of ribbon. We have noticed some with an insertion of guipure all round, and a white ribbon passed under it. The fronts and seams were stitched with white. The contrast is rather violent, and to some tastes may not be acceptable. Its originality is, perhaps, its principal recommendation. The buttons with which these paletots are ornamented have a white figure in the centre on a black ground.

* *
AUTHOR'S NOTE:

The daisy trimming sold by the yard in department stores would work up nicely. Cut at each joining and sew flowers to a piece of net to make the above described net.

* *

1860 PETERSON

LADY WASHINGTON CLOAK OF BLACK VELVET

TRIMMED WITH PASSEMENTERIE

PATTERN FOR A CHEMISE 1860 PETERSON

Thinking that a pattern of under-linen would be exceedingly acceptable to many of the subscribers to "Petersons", we, this month, give one of a chemise of the newest make. The back is straight, edged with a piece of work only; the front is trimmed with insertion, embroidery, and small tucks let in between the insertion. This trimming is of a pointed form; and the body of the chemise in front must be cut the same shape, to fit on this. The width of the long-cloth, or linen, is sufficient for the width of the garment, and should be gored at the top, the gores that are cut off being placed at the bottom, and the arm-hole shaped out. The sleeve is cut in two pieces, and should be joined together by a double row of stitching; it is made of Scotch cambric, with very small tucks run in it, to match the trimming in front. For strength and durability,

we would recommend that this be made of the same material as the chemise. As our space is limited, we have only been able to give, in the diagram, the half of both of the back and front, as far as the top of the gore; but the illustrations of the garments itself will clearly show how it should be made. The front is gathered from A to B; the part from A to the bottom of the point, and the same from B to C, being put on quite plain; it is gored from D to E, and the gore that comes off is put on to the bottom. The back of the chemise is plain from F to G; and the other portion of the back is gathered into the work on the top. It is gored from H to F; the gore that comes off being put on to the bottom, in the same manner as with the front gore.

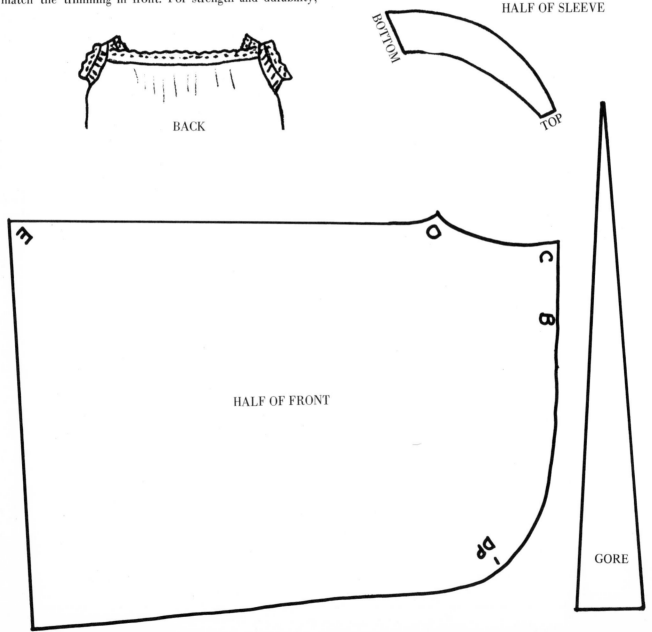

BACK

HALF OF SLEEVE

BOTTOM

TOP

HALF OF FRONT

GORE

PATTERN FOR A CHEMISE 1860 PETERSON

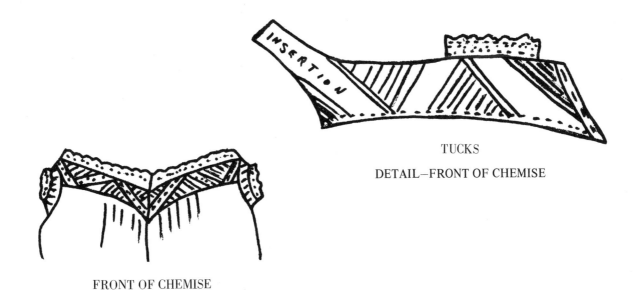

TUCKS

DETAIL—FRONT OF CHEMISE

FRONT OF CHEMISE

HALF OF BACK

LADIES NECKTIE LATEST STYLE 1860 PETERSON

Take a three-cornered piece of silk, lay four or five plaits on the bias side, until the point is only a little over a finger long. This point is to be embroidered, a bunch for a centre, (for which we give a very pretty pattern full size) and the sides are to be chain-stitched in blocks as seen in the design, sewing a small jet bead in the centre of every block. The dots on the strawberries are done in the same way. Fit the point to the neck, cutting off the ends in front. Edge all with a narrow black thread lace. Make a bow and ends for the front, embroidering the ends, and edging them with lace to match the point.

It is to be worn over a walking dress, with a very small linen collar, and may be made of any color to suit the dress or bonnet trimmings, always embroidered with black.

* *

AUTHOR'S NOTE:

The strawberry pattern is a full size pattern, but this collar tie can be duplicated for your doll's wardrobe by using a small transfer design of strawberries similar to the design shown.

Many small transfer designs are available in pattern departments in baby embroidery transfer packets. Also a small strawberry design may be found in children's coloring books.

* *

PETTICOAT TRIMS

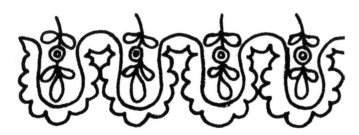

SILK EMBROIDERY ON FLANNEL

FOR BOTTOM OF PETTICOAT

1867 PETERSON EMBROIDERY PATTERNS

HANDKERCHIEF CORNER IN SATIN-STITCH

CORNER FOR COLLAR ON LINEN
IN SATIN-STITCH

HALF OF COLLAR AND CUFF

"NEW YEAR'S EVE"

JANUARY 1865 GODEY

As it is now out of the question to do without warm wraps, we will give our readers an idea of the most approved styles to be found in the show rooms.

Velvet wraps, which are considered the most elegant, are frequently made quite plain. When trimming is used, it is fur, guipure lace, or bead and crochet passementerie, and ornaments. The latter adorn every description of wrap this season.

The coat or paletot shape is the newest and most popular, though the ample rotunde is preferred by many and is quite admissable.

All wraps are made rather long, and frequently double breasted with revers, or button slanting from the shoulder to waist.

The jet and crochet ornaments are quite large, some resembling flowers, and are richer than ever before. Few hoods are worn on velvet cloaks this season.

Young ladies are wearing short loose sacks of a bright purple velvet cloth, trimmed with jet ornaments, or fringe formed of large worsted balls. This style of sack is both attractive and pretty. Thibet fringe of various colors is used on cloaks, and is one of the most elegant trimming introduced this season.

The most elegant opera cloaks are made of fleecy white cloth trimmed with Thibet fringe. Very full Thibet tassels are on the hood which should be lined with white silk.

We have seen some charming muslin skirts embroidered in high colors; others had rows of black braiding with bunches of tucks between. All very stylish and pretty to wear with a looped-up dress.

The new veils are rather peculiar in shape; they are quite narrow, almost oval, and the lower edge is perfectly straight. An elastic passes from one side of the lower edge to the other, and the veil fits closely to the face without rolling in at the sides, or pinning on top of the bonnet. They are generally formed of black and white spotted lace, and trimmed with either black or white chenille fringe. This style of veil is always very becoming.

Birds of all sizes are used in great profusion on most everything, and frequently the effect is both stylish and good.

There are some charming coiffures for young ladies. They consist of two tufts of flowers, one for the back and one for the front of the head joined by ribbons. A very graceful one was of silver wheat-ears mounted with thick stems of blue velvet tipped with silver. The two bunches were connected by blue velvet which fell in loops and ends at the back. Gold wheat was mounted with green velvet in the same way. Another very stylish head dress was of scarlet velvet with a cluster of thistles at the side, and a trailing branch of dark glossy leaves fell at the back.

The ball coiffures at this establishment are very lovely. Most of them consist of a large tuft with a garland falling loosely at the back, while soft thick stems are twined round the head, keeping the wreath in form. Thick stems of velvet are very much used; pink flowers are mounted on green velvet, and white flowers on blue or scarlet.

Butterflies continue to be popular ornaments, and are made of jet, gilt gauze, colored mother-of-pearl, and gauze lined with tinsel, while the more costly are studded with jewels.

In Paris two styles of bonnets are worn, the moderate and the tiny. The last are made up by some few milliners, but as yet are rather conspicuous for the street, and do not take well except for evening bonnets. When made of illusion with merely a fall of lace as a substitute for both crown and cape, it is really very difficult to distinguish them from a cap. We feel confident, however, that by spring none will be accepted but these mere caps. It is also rumored that bonnet strings are to be abandoned, and the bonnet is to be fastened on by the large Spanish pins, such as are now worn in the hair by young ladies.

A new style of comb has appeared for waterfalls. It is of ivory and perfectly straight and plain across the top over which the hair falls, but at the sides are large balls, having much the effect of the Spanish pins.

Buckles and belts daily increase in size, and are now so wide that they are very unsuitable for a short person. In order to make the belts fit without wrinkling it is necessary to have a plait in the back, and one under each arm; they then fit the figure closely. The buckles are very elegant, and in great variety. The gilt are the most stylish. Wide leather belts with ornamented leather buckles are very pretty for boys.

Long earrings are now the most fashionable; some consist of a double ball, others of a very long pendant.

Among the novelties just introduced in Paris are trimming braids, having on them heads of dogs, cats, horses, or stags. Horseshoes, cut out of leather and ornamented with steel knobs, are the employment for the trimming of ladies dresses.

Mme. Demerest has made quite an improvement in her dress elevators. It is no longer necessary to sew eyes on each breadth of the skirt to catch the hooks, as each string is now provided with little pin hooks which fasten the dress very gracefully. Some elevators have three pins to each string; these are thought to give the dress a better finish.

Every one knows how difficult it is to rip out machine sewing, particularly after it has been washed a few times; we would therefore mention that we saw at Mme. Demerest's a very simple little instrument expressly for ripping machine sewing.

Gored dresses are very much worn, frequently, however, the side breadths only are gored, which gives the dress a pretty sweep, without having that bare look we so often see in gored dresses.

Sashes are now wider than ever, and corsages of every description are worn. We have two very pretty corsages from the hands of Mme. Demerest, but the description of these with other matter will be obliged to reserve for another month.

THE ALEZANDRA.

Velvet mantle. trimmed with a deep guipure lace, and a wide guipure insertion with medallions. Round the neck is a hood formed of guipure. This style of mantle is fashionable for silks.

FEBRUARY 1865 GODEY

The corsages mentioned last month are the "Butterfly" and the "Regence". The former resembles the body of a butterfly, and has three points at the waist and three above. It laces up the back, and is very richly ornamented with jet and steel beads.

The "Regence" is a straight band laced at the back, and fastened in front with a large buckle. Two pieces cut like the lower part of a pointed waistcoat, commence at the hips, and widen as they approach the centre. A very great novelty, which we shall describe more for its eccentricity than its beauty, is the double-skirted dress. Imagine a gored skirt of scarlet poplin trimmed on the edge with a fluted ruffle, above which are four rows of black velvet. This may be regarded in the light of a petticoat. Over this is a dress of gray poplin with skirt slightly gored, and a plain, round corsage with very wide belt and buckle. The peculiarity of the dress is that the skirt is open from the waist to the edge of the skirt both back and front. It is furnished with buttons and buttonholes, so that it can be fastened up at pleasure. Rows of lace or velvet are carried all the way up the skirt on either side of the buttons and buttonholes. The belt, epaulettes, collar, and cuffs of the dress should match the underskirt in color and trimmings. In order to give our readers a better idea of this novelty, we will shortly give an illustration of it.

Looped dresses are still popular, and very pretty ornaments are now introduced for festooning them, such as bows of chenille with tassels, and fancy ornaments of steel, jet, velvet, and leather. Mixed goods are now very much worn for traveling dresses. They are made with mantles of the same, trimmed with ball fringe. Hoods are made to the mantles, as they are found very convenient to pull over the head as a substitute for a bonnet or hat in night traveling.

Besides the dress goods we have before mentioned, are striped silks, broad satin and silk stripes woven alternately, also embroidered silks, a large bouquet or design in each breadth. Some are very elegantly and elaborately embroidered with jet beads and bugles. For evening wear, there are very rich satins striped with velvet, and moires with designs in dead instead of bright silks, as in previous seasons, also small satin checks or spots with a large moire over them. Moires are also embroidered in lozenges and shaded figures; the most stylish, however, are branches of scarlet or white coral, on a pearl, black, blue, or white ground. Nothing, however, can exceed the richness of the plain moires, and in our eyes, they are far handsomer than any of the embroidered ones.

Owing to the high price of velvet this season, corded silk is very much used, and when trimmed with a profusion of jet ornaments makes a very elegant, and at the same time, expensive wrap.

One of the newest materials for sacks is called moufflon, and resembles sheepskin. The fleece is quite long and curly, and generally of a different color from the ground, such as gray on black ground, or white on a red, violet, or blue ground. The white, though adopted in Paris for street wear, is reserved here for opera cloaks or childrens wear, and for either purpose is extremely pretty and stylish. This moufflon is a very thick material, and should only be worn by a slender person. It is made up into short loose sacks with jackets in front, and trimmed with large buttons of smoked pearl, mother-of-pearl, or jet, as large as the base of a wine glass.

Silk cord is now very much used on the edge of dresses, but it is only suitable for a carriage or evening dress, as it rubs easily, and would not stand street wear.

Vests and jackets are very much worn, and coat sleeves only are admitted.

We are constantly questioned on the subject of crinoline— and though we frequently hear of its downfall, we see no diminution of it. The shape, however, is different. The newest style is very small, almost fitting the figure tightly, but directly in the back and half way down the skirt, a gore is inserted, which makes it quite ample round the edge, and gives the dress skirt a very graceful sweep.

The dressing of the hair is, of course, a subject of importance now that the back is no longer covered. The waterfall is the usual style, and as some persons may be at a loss to arrange it, we will give them a hint on the subject. Tie the back hair rather low on the neck, if a braid is required, tie it under the natural hair, letting it rest on the neck. Then roll the front hair and fasten the ends at the back. Comb the front locks, which are fastened at the back with the back hair. Pin on a frizette and turn the hair up over the comb, which must be entirely concealed. Then put on a net and tie a ribbon round the waterfall.

Another method of arranging a waterfall is to take a piece of net four inches long and three wide, sloping it off a little toward the upper part. On this piece sew rows of hair until it is sufficiently thick, then sew all on a small comb. After tucking your own hair into as small a space as possible, pin on a frizette. Then stick in your comb with the hair attached, and roll the ends underneath and fasten with hairpins. Cover with a net and tie a ribbon round. This makes a very pretty waterfall, and will also answer for Grecian curls. Any ordinary pointed braid can be ripped up and arranged as described. The hair is still rolled in front, and frequently the parting of the hair is hidden by rolls or a bunch of curls. A very good illustration of this style of coiffure will be found in our fashion plate.

Another style of arranging the back of hair is in two loops, one above the other. Three rows of narrow velvet are worn round the head, and looped in with the loops of hair. Tulle is greatly in favor for the hair and neck; it also takes the place of the wide ribbon sashes.

As hints on the trimming of underclothing are sometimes acceptable, we would suggest, to those who do not care to embroider their flannel skirts, to cut them in scollops and bind them with a bias strip of colored flannel. Fold each breadth in eight, pin it firmly, and cut in a half circle. This will be found a good plan for cutting scallops.

White muslin ties are in great favor. Some are quite long, and are tucked in the dress at about the fourth button from the top.

NEW STYLE OF OPEN DRESS.

New style of open dress, described in the February chat. Scarlet petticoat, trimmed with a deep fluted ruffle and four rows of black velvet. Dress of silver gray poplin, trimmed with black guipure lace, narrow black velvet, and jet buttons. The front of the skirt is trimmed the same as the back. Scarlet belt, collar, cuffs, and epaulettes all trimmed with bands of black velvet.

COIFFURES

(See page 67 for description.)

KNITTED HOOD,
WITH SWANS'DOWN BORDER.

EVENING DRESS.

MARCH 1865 GODEY

So great is the variety in materials, trimmings and in the styles of making dresses, bonnets, and wraps, that it is almost impossible to say what is really the fashion. Everything is worn; no two garments are made alike. A few general rules prevail as to shape, but the trimming are varied according to the taste and genius of the artistic wearer.

Something new and stylish in the way of morning dresses is the gored underskirt of white alpaca, trimmed on the edge with a fluted ruffle bound with black velvet. A vest of white alpaca is buttoned to the throat with square mother-of-pearl and jet buttons. Over this is a robe of violet cashmere of the redingote style, that is gored, and cut into the figure, but not fitting it tightly. This dress is quite short only reaching the top of the ruffle on the petticoat. It is finished with a fluted ruffle of the cashmere, headed by a brilliant band of Persian bordering, which is also carried up the front. The corsage is fastened at the waist and at the throat, showing the vest in between.

Puffed skirts of illusion on tarletane are always in demand, as there is nothing so graceful and pretty for a young person as a thin dress. In order to give them more firmness, they should be puffed on a skirt of stiff net or thin, stiff muslin. This should be gored to fit the figure tightly over the hips, in order not to have any plaits at the waist, as they would interfere greatly with the puffs, which however, should be almost plain at the waist. Over these puffed skirts is frequently worn a skirt of tulle without hem; this is termed a veil, and adds lightness to the dress. When the puffings run lengthwise, they should be graduated, and if expense is not feared, they can be separated by garlands of flowers, or studded over with butterflies of bright-colored crepe or blonde. Blonde flowers are also much used for ornamenting and looping up thin evening dresses.

Lace scarfs, arranged over the chest in the order style, are very much in vogue. So also are bows of ribbon, illusion, or black lace with long streamers fastened on the left shoulder. This style of bow is also worn on paletots, and we think will be very popular for the spring silk wraps.

The newest style of belt is of black gimp and beads, with a large buckle to match. The advantages of this style of belt is that it can be worn with any dress. Aumonieres or small bags to wear at the side for the purse or handkerchief, are to be had of gimp and jet, to match the belts.

Many of the sashes are tied at the left side. Others are caught with a large buckle in front, and tie at the back with large bows and ends. Cashmere sashes are worn over morning robes, and are fastened at the back with a large bow.

Light silks are frequently trimmed with silk of the same color but of a much darker shade, arranged in ruffles, medallions, or in some fanciful style. Moires and heavy silk are frequently slit up to the waist on each side, and a gore of white silk, handsomely trimmed, is let in. Thick silk cord is one of the richest trimmings for a heavy silk. A pretty method of arranging it is to have six or seven rows, slightly waved, running round the skirt. These are festooned half way up on the left side of the skirt, with loops of cord and Thibet tassels.

The newest style of quilting petticoats is black silk, cut in narrow gores about a quarter of a yard wide. Each gore is piped with a bright-colored silk or braid, and the skirt is bound with a braid matching the pipings in color.

The latest hoop skirts are made with hoops commencing below the hips. These are connected with the belt by wide tapes. This style of skirt will be found very becoming to persons with large hips.

APRIL 1865 GODEY

The mania for butterflies seems to be on the increase. They are now the fashionable trimming for dresses, coiffures, caps, bonnets, collars, and cuffs.

Plain linen collars and cuffs are still very much worn. The collars are small, some quite round, others have pointed fronts. The more dressy ones are made with short tabs in front trimmed with Valenciennes, while a design of the same lace is appliqued over the linen. A butterfly or bee of lace is frequently inserted in the thick linen collars with admirable effect.

Undersleeves are made with a deep cuff either tight at the wrist, or loose enough to pass the hand through. The sleeves should be of the coat shape, in order to fit well under the dress sleeves, which are now too small to admit of a very full under-sleeve without giving the arm a stuffed appearance.

A novelty in lingerie is the Queen Bess ruff. It consists of a double fluted ruffle the lower one three inches deep, and the upper one which stands up round the neck about three quarters of an inch deep. They are generally made of French muslin, and many of them are perfectly plain, while others are prettily trimmed with Valenciennes lace. They vary in price from fifty cents to four dollars, according to the ornamentation. Very pretty ones can be had trimmed suitably for mourning.

Beads enter largely into the decorations of the present day, and when artistically mounted, are really effective and beautiful. Some are quite costly, being of malacite, pink or red coral, amber, and frosty-looking crystal. All these are employed for head dresses, particularly for the trimming of nets. The more showy and elaborate kinds form the most effective coiffures. They are generally very large, and adorned with immense pearl, jet, steel, or crystal beads. The most elegant have a double row of beads forming a coronet in front, while a fringe of beads with pendant ends falls at the back.

Another pretty novelty is the velvet jewelry. These comprise necklaces, bracelets, earrings, buckles, and combs, formed of balls, chains, and grelots of blue or scarlet or black velvet caught and fastened with gilt and pearl ornaments. This velvet jewelry is extremely pretty and effective with white dresses, and very suitable for a young lady.

Gored walking dresses are becoming exceedingly fashionable. A very stylish one was of black and green linsey woolsey, looped up with broad bands of gimp worked with jet and trimmed with fringe.

A new finish for white bodies is ribbon velvet, on which are fastened small flowers. This style of decoration is placed round the throat and wrists. A bright blue velvet, edged with lace and dotted with very small roses, has a charming effect.

It is said that a radical change is soon to take place in fashions. Crinoline is to be discarded, skirts to be gored, almost tight to the figure, and very short. Waists are also to be short, and heart-shaped in front, and worn with wide belts and large buckles. We give this merely as an ondit; we think the costumes of our grandmothers are not likely to be adopted very soon by us.

We have lately seen some very charming materials for ball dresses. Some of the prettiest were tarletanes of delicate shades of blue, buff, and pink, on which were elaborate designs formed of a kind of silver band. Others were of tulle, on which butterflies, bees, and flies seemed to be resting. Others were of white tarletane brocaded with buttercups, roses, and daisies in the richest shades.

The latest Parisian novelty, in the way of a bonnet, is called the mantilla bonnet. It is generally formed of some light material, such as white puffed tulle, dotted over with bugles, and trimmed with flowers glistening with dew drops. The crown is soft and covered with blonde, which is prolonged into pelerine covering the shoulders. This is extremely graceful, coquettish coiffure, but only fit for evening wear.

MAY 1865 GODEY

At this season of the year, when persons are obliged to make additions to their wardrobes, a few hints respecting the making up of goods is generally acceptable.

With regard to dresses, we may confidently state that double skirts will be worn in thin materials. Cut skirts, so much in vogue a few years ago, have again revived, and are in great favor for organdies and other wash goods. The skirt is cut off just below the knee, and two extra breadths are allowed for the lower part. The upper edge of the lower half of the skirt is hemmed, a cord is run in to form a ruffle, and the deep flounce is then readjusted to finish the skirt. This same style is very suitable for barege or silk goods, and the joining is generally concealed by a fluting or puffing of ribbon silk.

The most convenient style of corsage for wash goods is to have a little fullness at the waist, plain on the shoulders, and made up without any lining whatever. This of course necessitates a nice corset cover, and we have lately seen a very convenient and simple pattern just brought out by Mme. Demerest. The back is a plain basque, the front is also a basque, but has a little fullness at the waist. It is of course low on the neck, and finished with a short sleeve formed of a single puff. The advantage of this basque is that the body can be kept in place by skirt bands.

Drawn waists are also being made up for wash dresses. In some the cords run lengthwise, and in others across.

Tarletane is a favorite material for thin waists, and is exceedingly light and pretty either puffed or drawn with cords. Tall persons are wearing round bodices with wide waistbands and buckles, but short persons had better avoid them, as they have the effect of shortening the waist. A new style of waist has appeared with broad bands and buckles on the top of the sleeves, and at the lower edge of the sleeves, as well as round the waist.

For rich silks made with double skirts, the latest style is to have the body and upper skirt in one piece. They are gored to fit the waist without pleats, and are exceedingly wide round the edge of the skirt.

Looking over the large collections of patterns just made by Mme. Demerest, we noticed the sleeves to be rigorously of the coat-shape, but trimmed in many novel and pretty styles suitable both for wash and other goods. Cords and tassels trim very many of the spring sleeves, and as very pretty ones can be obtained of cotton, they can be used on wash dresses.

Some new patterns for bodices have appeared. One very suitable for silk or travelling dress goods, is made to button down the shoulder and slanting from the shoulder to the waist. On each side of the front is a tiny pocket, and at the back is a very pretty and fanciful tail, which can be trimmed plainly or richly to suit the taste of the wearer.

There are two styles of alpaca this season, the glace and the plain. They are of good quality and new shades, and we know of no nicer material for a travelling dress or a demi-toilette than an alpaca.

The mohairs are mostly of broken and plain checks of all the pretty spring colors, and the much admired black and white combinations. The new piques and organdies are extremely fresh and beautiful both in colors and designs. We see light green, China-blue, leather color, maize and violet striped with white. Others are figured with lovers knots, lace designs, angles, triangles, feathers, lozenges, diamonds, squares, linked rings, fox heads, bouquets, horseshoes, butterflies, bugs, birds, parallel lines, Grecques, and every other imaginable design. Some of these devices are small and dotted over the material; others are very large, and form borderings and tablier patterns for robes. The body is printed to match the skirt, and frequently a shawl or sack, also printed to match, comes to complete the suit.

A pretty style for making up a pique is to have the corsage made with short points behind and before, and a row of loops formed of black alpaca braid, arranged close together and falling over the skirt as a fringe. The same trimming can be repeated around the throat. The braid should be soaked in warm water, constantly renewed for a day to prevent the dye staining the dress.

The assortment of cambrics this season is particularly good. We noticed one of a white ground with black squares scattered over it, which was exceedingly effective. In thin wool goods, we notice cloudy silky grounds with large silk spots of a bright color, contrasting well with the gray ground.

Besides the ever fashionable spring checked silks of the daintiest colors, there are others of delicate shades of green, blue, or violet, shot with white.

Another style of silk of very rich quality is studded with bright stars peeping through grayish-looking clouds, dashed with bright streaks. Other silks have feathers, butterflies, or wheat-ears thrown over them.

The most elegant grenadines are of white grounds with gorgeous butterflies of life size fitting over them.

Among the spring novelties in lingerie, are some new handkerchiefs having corner pieces and borders formed of alternate blocks of pink and white cambric neatly stitched on. Mauve, black, and blue are also most gracefully combined in other styles.

The most attractive novelties, however, are wreaths of black lace representing flowers tied with a bow and ends. They are intended for the trimming of dresses, one wreath for each breadth. On a maize, violet, white, or pink silk, nothing could be more effective and stylish.

Black lace medallions have also been brought out for parasols. These are laid on each division of the parasol, which should be covered with white or some very light color. They are much more beautiful than the entire covers of former seasons.

The new gloves are of very light shades, quite high on the wrist, and finished with a pinked scallop.

The latest tie is about a yard long and three inches wide. It is formed of gauze, blue, for instance, with a white stripe on each edge and ends heavily fringed with white and blue. Others brilliant with beads and bugles, and finished with rich tasseled ends, are very fashionable.

The pompadour style of head dress is very generally adopted by young ladies. A very large graduated rat or roll is laid over the front of the head, and the hair is brushed over it a la Chinoise. To many this style of coiffure is exceedingly becoming. The hair is sometimes crimped and arranged in the same style.

What we should term the horse-tail style has been adopted by a few young ladies (and we are happy to say but by very few) for evening wear. The front hair is either rolled or dressed a la Pompadour, and the back is tied with a bright ribbon, and allowed to fall unrestrained over the shoulders. Flowing locks read well in poetry, and sometimes look well in a picture, but for an evening party they are positively disgraceful.

Fancy ball pins of every description are worn. One ball is fastened to the pin and the other attached to an elastic, which is taken off to allow the pin to go through the hair, and then readjusted to fasten it. Combs of fanciful styles continue to be worn, and among the new ones we saw some having three long, feather-like pieces of mother-of-pearl arranged as a Scotch plume, and caught on to the gilded top of the comb by a jewel.

Talking of jewels, we know of no fashionable ornament more devoided of beauty than the rock crystal earrings now exhibited. They remind one of the pendents attached to the old-fashioned glass chandeliers, and are no prettier. We cannot imagine they can be at all popular. Long earrings do not seem to take well here, though made up in very beautiful and quaint designs.

Bonnets are now but mere handkerchiefs trimmed with flowers and ribbons. Straws have also appeared minus crowns.

JUNE 1865 GODEY

The new color known as "moon on the lake", we think a very poetical but inappropriate title. It is a very rich, lovely shade of pearl-color, and nothing more. This shade is extremely fashionable, and can be had in ribbons, silks, crepes, feathers, and flowers.

There is a handsome assortment of goods in mohair lace that we have seen. So fine are the laces, and so exquisite the designs, that, unless very closely examined, they cannot be detected from thread lace. They are no common imitations, but are really exquisite articles. Some of the rotondes, or circles, are exceedingly long, others are of moderate length. They are made up to suit the most capricious tastes, some with round, full hoods, others with square yokes, or else perfectly plain with square rounded ends in front. Besides these rotondes, are the graceful half shawls or points as they are termed, always fashionable and pretty. Shawls and circles are also to be had of white mohair lace.

For the ornamentation of dresses there are bunches of wheat-ears in black lace, medallions, Bayadere trimmings, and long graduated sashes to hang all round the skirt, and various other fanciful designs. As these goods are all of mohair lace, they are much less expensive than the thread, and the effect at a short distance is equally as good. For wash dresses, there is a thread lace resembling Valenciennes, which has the merit of washing and wearing well, and being about half the price of the ordinary Valenciennes.

For neglige wear there are shetland of all styles and colors, also coverings for the head.

Nets of all kinds are worn. Some of the newest are covered with steel or gilt spangles, or else large crystal beads. The present mania seems to be for beads and glittering trimmings of all descriptions. Cover your dresses, cloaks, and dark bonnets with jet, steel, gilt, or fancy colored beads. Pour over your evening dresses, bonnets, neck ties, flowers and plumes, any quantity of dew-drops, icicles, rain-drops, crystal and satin beads, and you will be a la mode.

In lieu of the net, some married ladies have adopted a bag of bright silk or velvet, either plain or ornamental with beads. These are drawn into the form of a net by an elastic, and fastened to a comb, taking the place of the waterfall. It is a convenient and dressy style of coiffure and as the bag can be stuffed with a roll of horse-hair, it is of but little consequence if Nature has been sparing of her gifts.

The latest novelty for the hair consists of bows and curls of spun gold. Hummingbirds and flies are still worn in the hair, also snow-white butterflies striped with scarlet or gold.

Among the novelties we find the becoming little Spanish square for the head, in point applique; also square capes, a pretty and stylish finish to the low-necked dresses now so much worn. The capeline is a pointed cape in black lace, with hood attached, a very dressy little affair for a watering-place.

Bonnets are exceedingly small, but what is wanting in quantity is made up for in quality, all the materials being of the finest, choicest kinds, and thoroughly Parisian. Though trimming is lavishly used, it is hardly required, so fanciful and decorative are the delicate chips; the pretty Italian and fine English straws, not to mention the Neapolitans, which form the daintiest basket and filagree work, dotted with small crystal, pearl, or jet beads.

Straw cloth, a mixture of Leghorn and silk, constitutes some of the most effective and stylish bonnets. They are frequently ornamented with a delicate embroidery of beads, and trimmed with a narrow ribbon of the same material as the bonnet; worked with scarlet, black, blue, or purple. Flowers are gracefully entwined, and the combination is generally a very great success. These straw ribbons are also much used for the trimming of round hats, and also border the most expensive styles of silk ribbons.

Bonnets are of different shapes; some are only a half handkerchief of silk or straw, others have short, sloping crowns. The first style is donned by young ladies, or of coiffure. The shapes are close, some fitting the face almost like a cap, and admitting of but little face trimming. Curtains are ignored by all, though in many the space accorded to the latter is filled by a fall of lace, or feather fringe. The half-handkerchief bonnets are generally trimmed with clustering loops of ribbon with very long ends, flowers, or scarfs of illusion edged with narrow blonde lace. Sometimes there are but two streamers of ribbon, which are caught together a short distance below the bonnet by a bow. A pretty style consists of two scarfs or strips of illusion half a yard wide, and three quarters long. These are caught inside of the front of the bonnet, pass over it, and are fastened just over the waterfall with a tuft of flowers, or a mother-of-pearl butterfly, star, or fancy ornament.

Others have very long tulle streamers to fasten under the chin. Nothing can be lighter and prettier than these scarfs thrown over a tulle or crepe bonnet. They are perishable, we admit, but exceedingly light and graceful, and can be renewed at a trifling expense.

A new style of straw bonnet has the straw pressed out in diamonds, which gives the effect of tufting, each little pearl, crystal, or jet bead.

A very original bonnet in fine English straw, is embroidered on the edge in a delicate bead pattern. At the back two crimped straw puffs, ornamented with brilliant blue enamelled insects, form a waterfall. This is surmounted by white ribbon brocaded in the centre in green, scarlet, and black. Scarlet poppies with jet, fancy grass and narrow quilling of black lace complete the decorations of the bonnet.

A very beautiful Italian straw is trimmed with a fall of green feather fringe at the back, and lovely transparent straw ornaments. Chains formed of straw are caught in festoons, and hang quite low on the neck. The ribbon is striped straw-color and green, and has the appearance of fine silk canvas.

Drawn silk bonnets are greatly in favor for travelling. The drawings are far apart, not more than three being used. They are generally finished by a pinked-out rose quilling of the silk, and loops of ribbon arranged at the back of the bonnet. The ruche is graduated, being quite large in centre, and forms a very good apology for a curtain. Bonnets both with and without crowns, are made in this style. Colored straws trimmed with ribbon to match, are also in high favor.

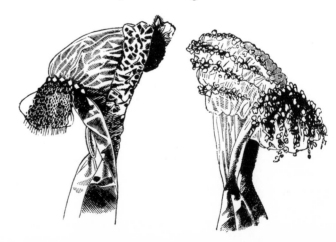

The snowflake, like tulle bonnets, are always attractive and we think them among the prettiest for summer wear. They are generally puffed lengthwise, and ornamented with tulle scarfs, which we have already described, and very rich flowers, with frosted or icy foliage. Falls of silk fringe are also employed with good effect. The strings generally commence at the point of the waterfall and are thence brought down under the chin. So shallow are the shapes, that the strings almost form the sides of the bonnet.

Crepe is very much worn, fulled or folded over silk. When the bonnet is thin, the front is generally bound an inch deep with silk matching the crepe. Crepe, and crepelisse, matching the bonnet in color, are both employed for inside ruchings.

To describe all the exquisite models brought out at the Maison Tilman, would be an endless theme. We give merely the newest ideas and what we think will be useful and practical to our readers.

One of the newest styles is a Scotch cap with a melon-shaped crown made of light scalloped-edged straw, the indenture in the crown being very deep. Another shape, termed the Cracovienne, has a square crown. Another shape still is a full round crown with narrow brim, the same size all round. The cap shape, however, seems to be the most popular with young ladies. There are, of course, many other very graceful shapes, but those we have mentioned we think will be the most fashionable, as they are made up in all sizes from babies to ladies. A novelty, however, consists in cutting away one-half the crown, and filling in the space with black lace finished with ribbons and flowers. Another variation of this style has quite a long, drooping crown of lace; this we do not like. It is a kind of a compromise between a bonnet and hat, and not very pretty.

Another hat, called the Havelock has the crown cut away and a very long bag crown of colored silk attached, in which the hair is arranged. This is more novel than pretty, but would answer very well for a travelling hat, as the waterfall would be protected from the dust.

The most elegant trimmings are black and white ribbons, brocaded on the edge or down the centre, in a rich cashmere pattern. Heavy ribbons with scalloped edges fringed scarfs of black lace, jet straw, and enamel ornaments; flowers and feathers also Brazilian beetles, in their peculiar and brilliant shade of green. This shade of green has also been introduced in a few ribbon and feather ornaments for round hats.

BONNETS.
(See Description, Fashion Department.)

Buttons are extensively used as decorations, and never have we seen such an elegant variety. Some are the size of small bird's eggs, of blue, brown, white, or black, spanned by a band of gold or steel. Others resemble a cluster of tiny pearls, or a single pearl the size of a pea. Flat, round, and square buttons of mother-of-pearl, crystal, or a material resembling white onyx, with a bar of gold or jet across them, or else having a small gilt ornament in the centre, are also among the newest. Other novel styles are of jet or pearl, strapped across with narrow bands of bright-colored braid, or else have a mosaic figure in the centre.

The ornaments are generally on the shoulders and up the back, in a pyramidal form. Steel is very much worn on dresses, and though worn in Paris on wraps, does not take well here. The combination of jet and silk is generally preferred, as it is rich and less conspicuous than steel.

SLEEVE TRIMMING IN FLANDERS LACE 1865 GODEY

MATERIALS: A steel netting mesh, No. 9; and crochet cotton, No. 16, for the grounding; Cotton No. 7, No. 8 ditto, and No. 30 will be used for working the pattern.

The ground is here represented as scalloped, but it will be better to make a straight piece of netting, and cut out the scallops afterwards. Begin with one stitch, as for square netting, and work backwards for forwards, increasing, by doing two stitches in one, at the end of every row, until there are 29 holes up one side, and 30 up the other. Do one row without increase or decrease; increase the next as usual; but at the end of the following row take two stitches together. Repeat these two rows—that is, increasing at the end of one,

and decreasing at the end of the other, until up the straight side you have as great a length as you require, taking care that it shall be sufficient for complete patterns. Do another row without increase or decrease and finish by netting two stitches together at the end of every row, till the piece comes to a point.

The piece for each sleeve may be made separately or not. When the netting is finished, it must be washed, slightly stiffened, and pinned out to dry in proper shape. Then tack it on toile circee, and darn it according to the pattern.

The wheels are to be button-holed over a double thread run round in the proper shape, as seen in the engraving. For this, No. 16 cotton will do. The loops that form the crosses in the wheels are done in No. 7 cotton. The cloth-darning, that is the darning in which four threads cross each other in every square—is done in 80 cotton. On referring to the engraving, it will be seen that these lines are continuous where two or more squares joining together are darned in the same way. The threads should fall alternately under and over each other; and this will do so if in whatever direction you darn, you never cross over more than one thread, whether of the ground net or the darning. This rule must be observed even in turning a corner.

The plain white line that surrounds all this darning is an outline with the coarse cotton, an occasional twist round the corner of a square being given to it to keep it in its place. The upper part of the pattern, with all those squares filled by plain white lines, are closely darned in embroidery cotton.

This will be found a very simple and effective style of work, much richer than any ordinary embroidery, as well as more easily executed.

SLEEVE TRIMMING IN FLANDERS LACE

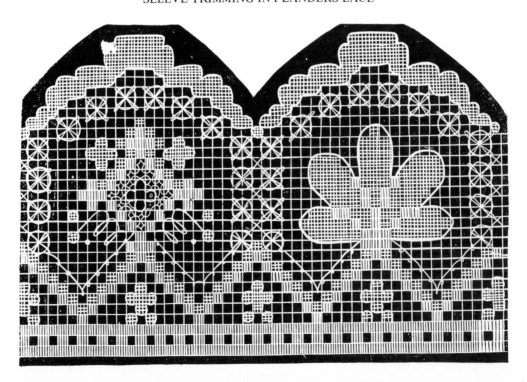

* *

AUTHOR'S NOTE:

   This Flanders lace would make a most attractive trim for a doll's dress. Use the width shown for the dress hem or for a petticoat and develop a narrower version for the sleeve. Trace the pattern on tissue of the required length, pin the tissue to a piece of net, and embroider the design on the net for an authentic 1865 lace trim.

* *

THE ANDALUSIAN JACKET 1865 GODEY
(FITS 11½" HIGH HEEL DOLLS)

   Among the many new patterns of Spanish jackets, that we give, called the Andalusian, is one of the most stylish. These jackets continue as fashionable as ever. To be made of silk, and worn with a muslin skirt for morning and home costume, or as the dress body for thin silks and foulards. It is composed of the front, side-piece, and back of the jacket, and the front of the waistcoat, which is distinguished by a rounded shape, the waistcoat buttons from top to bottom. The shoulder and side-seams are sewn in with the shoulder and side-seams of the jacket. The jacket closes at the throat and is rounded well off, forming a skirt about six inches deep at the back, which is finished by two plaits.

* *

AUTHOR'S NOTE:

   Stitch jacket front darts, vest darts, sew side-body back to jacket back, forming the plaits as described above. Stitch front and vest shoulder seams to back jacket shoulder seams; sew side seams. Sew or embroider trimmings. Line all pieces.

* *

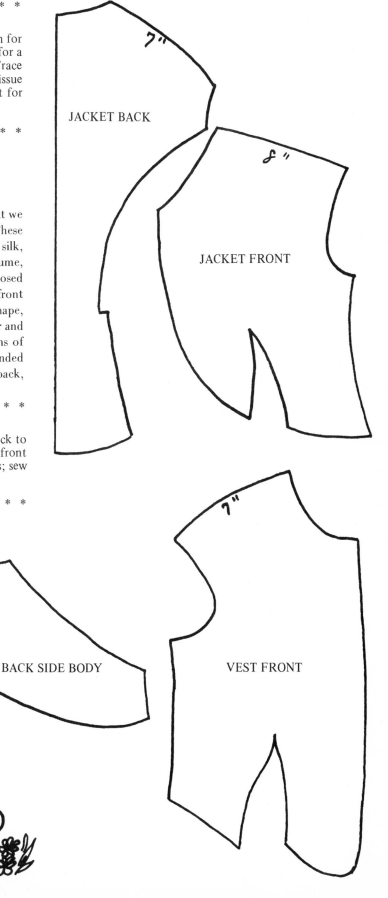

JACKET BACK

JACKET FRONT

BACK SIDE BODY

VEST FRONT

EMBROIDERY DESIGNS 1865 GODEY

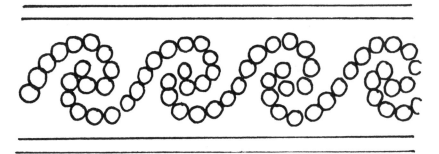

EMBROIDERY DESIGN

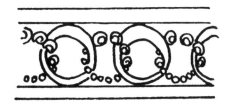

BRAID DESIGN

EMBROIDERY DESIGN

BRAID DESIGN

BRAID DESIGN

BRAIDING PATTERN

EMBROIDERY DESIGNS 1865 GODEY

EMBROIDERY DESIGN

BUTTERFLY EMBROIDERY

BRAID EMBROIDERY DESIGN

EMBROIDERY DESIGN

EMBROIDERY FOR SKIRT

BRAID TRIMMINGS FOR UNDERLINEN, JACKETS,
CHILDREN'S THINGS 1865 GODEY

Embroidered trimmings requiring infinite time and trouble to work, and lace ones being very expensive, they are now replaced by patterns worked in black or colored braid, and fastened on the right side of the material with cross stitches. The braid is arranged either in straight lines or vandykes, the intervals being embroidered in chain stitch or point russe with butterfly knots, stars, crosses, and a variety of other small patterns. We give two illustrations of this kind of trimming which our lady readers will find extremely easy to copy, and which will be very useful for Zouave jackets, petticoats, chemisettes, and children's frocks. For washing materials the braid should be white, put on with colored cotton or silk.

Braid Trimming For A Morning Dress —This trimming is made of a new and very fine description of cordon braid, the size and make of which is correctly given in our illustration. Trace the pattern and tack it on the dress, sew on the braid and tear the paper away. This braid is most suited to washing dresses but may be used for any light material.

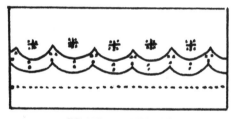

BRAID TRIMMING

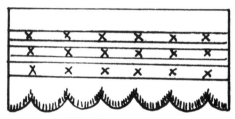

BRAID TRIMMING

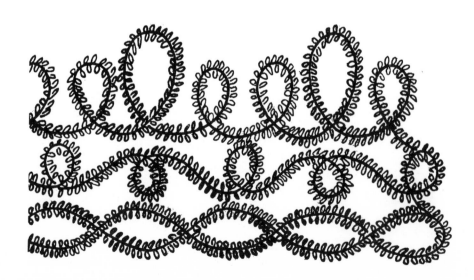

BRAID TRIMMING FOR MORNING DRESS

BEAD BUTTERFLY FOR DRESS ORNAMENT
1865 GODEY

This butterfly is meant for an ornament in dress, and can be placed in the center of a rosette of ribbon or lace, or of a bunch of flowers. To make it, begin by cutting out the shape represented at the lower corner of the opposite engraving. Cut it out in cardboard, and cover it entirely with black silk, then pass a piece of black silk through the whole length of the body. One end of this silk is used to thread the beads, the other to fasten them on. First arrange one row of beads round the edge of the body, then thread as many beads as will cover the width of it, and fasten them on by inserting the needle through one of the beads at the edge. Repeat the same process for the opposite side, and continue in the same way until the body is completely covered. If you wish the butterfly's back to be rounded a little, you have only to fasten a few wool ends along the top before putting on the beads. The long feelers are imitated by two bits of wire with a bead at the top; the short ones by three beads, threaded on wire; the eyes by larger beads. A long piece of wire forms the stems of the winged flower. The wings are very easy to make from the illustration. The beads are threaded on very fine wire. When the two large loops A and B are finished, the smaller ones are begun over the first. This loop A is joined on to the other at the point by a bead and two more small loops are then added. All the ends of wire must be joined on to the principal stem. After the wings are joined on to the body, five loops should be made and fastened on through a bead; the middle one has two smaller loops formed at the point. The wire stem is wrapped over with a very narrow piece of silk cut the cross way. The color of the beads can be chosen according to taste.

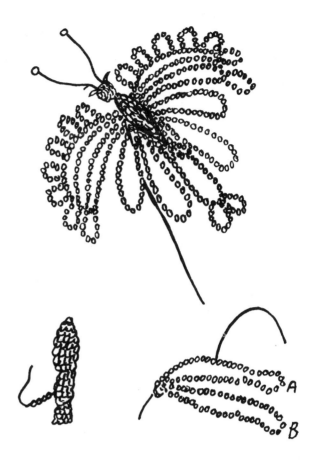

DRESS TRIMMING IN SILK 1865 GODEY

This trimming is more particularly suitable for a silk dress, but may also be employed for one of merino or fancy woolen material. Our illustration shows part of it in full size. It is composed of stripes of silk placed at small distances one from another, and joined at the top and bottom by a narrow strip of the same material; the edges are stitched in black. A slit is cut out to about half-way in each of the wide strips (see illustration). To make the rosettes, take a piece of silk pinked out round the edge one inch wide and eight inches long; begin by making one double pleat in the centre, then take two on each side. These pleats must be folded so as to be narrow at the bottom and wide at the top, which forms the rosette quite naturally. The rosette is placed over the strip, and the sides folded back inside the slit and secured on the wrong side. This trimming looks pretty when made of a color contrasting with that of the material of the dress which shows between the openings.

* *
AUTHOR'S NOTE:
   Make one-half inch wide for doll dress trim.

* *

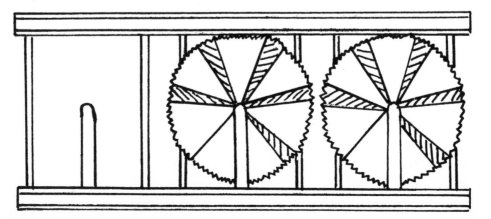

BABY'S SHOE 1865 GODEY
(WILL FIT CHARMIN' CHATTY)

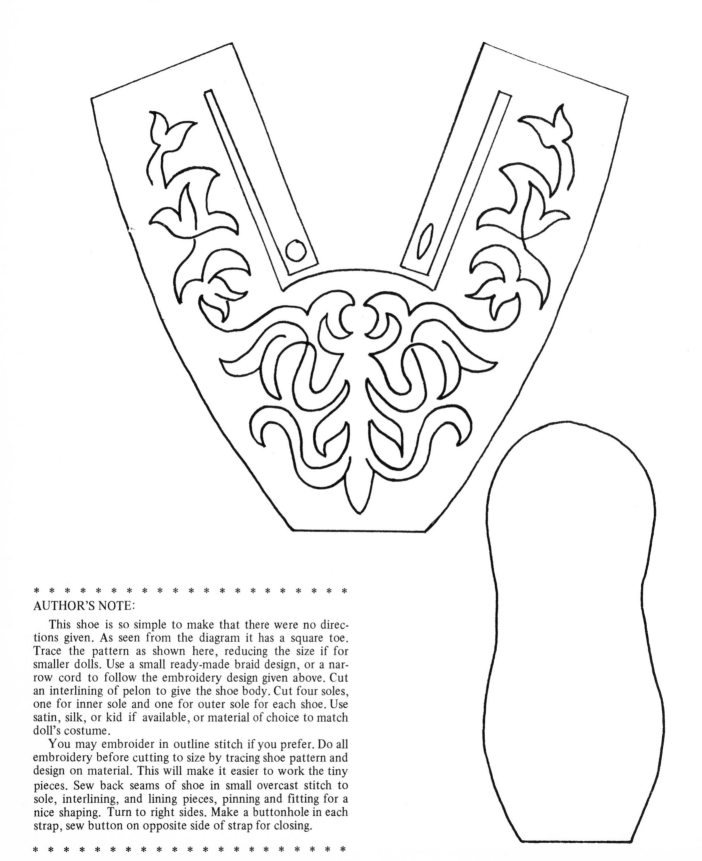

* *

AUTHOR'S NOTE:

This shoe is so simple to make that there were no directions given. As seen from the diagram it has a square toe. Trace the pattern as shown here, reducing the size if for smaller dolls. Use a small ready-made braid design, or a narrow cord to follow the embroidery design given above. Cut an interlining of pelon to give the shoe body. Cut four soles, one for inner sole and one for outer sole for each shoe. Use satin, silk, or kid if available, or material of choice to match doll's costume.

You may embroider in outline stitch if you prefer. Do all embroidery before cutting to size by tracing shoe pattern and design on material. This will make it easier to work the tiny pieces. Sew back seams of shoe in small overcast stitch to sole, interlining, and lining pieces, pinning and fitting for a nice shaping. Turn to right sides. Make a buttonhole in each strap, sew button on opposite side of strap for closing.

* *

COIFFURE DIADEM 1865 GODEY

Coiffure Astree. The coiffure is formed of rose-colored velvet, covered with a fringe of pearl beads. In front is a long white plume, loops of rose-colored velvet, and leaves of mother-of-pearl.

FANCY GIRDLE 1865 GODEY

Girdle with three streamers of blue silk. The ends are braided with black cord, and trimmed with black chenille tassels.

SLEEVES OF 1865 GODEY

Fig. 1.   Fancy undersleeve, with a butterfly embroidered
in bright colors.

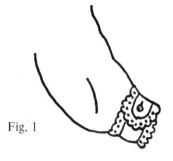

Fig. 1

Fig. 2.   Muslin undersleeve, with fancy puffed cuff with
deep Valenciennes lace.

Fig. 2

Fig. 3.   Fancy linen cuff, embroidered with butterflies.

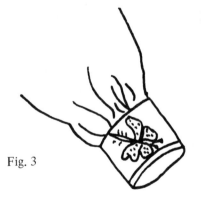

Fig. 3

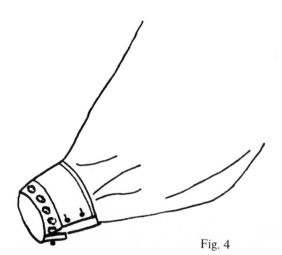

Fig. 4.   A new style of linen cuff, embroidered with small
butterflies in bright colors.

Fig. 4

THE MARGUERITE GIRDLE 1865 GODEY

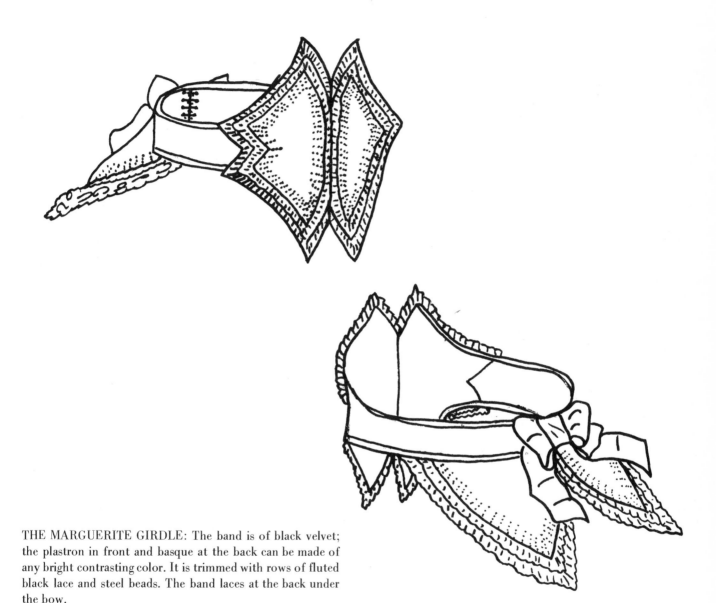

THE MARGUERITE GIRDLE: The band is of black velvet; the plastron in front and basque at the back can be made of any bright contrasting color. It is trimmed with rows of fluted black lace and steel beads. The band laces at the back under the bow.

* * * * * * * * * * * * * * * * * * *

AUTHOR'S NOTE:

    To make this girdle take the waist measurement of the doll to be dressed, trace and cut the plastron pattern from lightweight cardboard, and cover with your choice of material and lining; decorate as shown. The basque and back can be cut in the shape shown and made to fit the band. Plastron fronts and basque back are finished and trimmed to match the dress. The band can also be cut of lightweight cardboard, covered with velvet, then lined and edged with piping. Punch holes with a small awl for the back lacing of soutache braid or narrow cord. Make a bow and sew in place with snaps for easy removal.

* * * * * * * * * * * * * * * * * * *

THE ADOLPHE COAT
AUGUST 1864 PETERSON
(FITS 4½" CHINA HEAD CLOTH BODY DOLLS)

Our illustration of this very novel and stylish garment so clearly depicts the arrangement of it that an explanation is scarcely necessary. In Paris for the last few weeks, both high and low coats have been much worn. Our pattern consists of seven pieces: the front, the back, the side-piece, that fits into the back; the sleeves; the revers for the basque or tail behind; the collar. A row of tiny dashes on the sleeve indicates the upper and under portion, the smallest piece being for the under part. The pattern is cut to fit a medium-sized figure, and it can easily be enlarged or diminished by cutting each piece larger or smaller, as may be required. For a very elegant garment, the revers should be in white silk, strapped with black velvet, but if required for a more useful style silk the same as the dress, or black silk, may be employed. The front of the coat is like a dress bodice, open a little in front, and ornamented with a revers which is carried round the arms and ends in the revers on the basque. A tiny collar finishes the top of the dress behind and just meets the revers in front. By consulting the diagram, our readers will experience no difficulty in putting the various pieces together. The back is shown with three stars, indicating the center. The side-piece is numbered 1, to correspond with fig. 1 on the back. The front is numbered under the arm, and fits into the side-piece to the corresponding fig. 2. The revers for back is numbered 1, and must be placed exactly over the figures 1 of side-piece and back. The front revers joins the two letters A to the back revers, and the collar meets the revers at B. From this diagram giving the patterns on a small scale, cut full-sized patterns.

BURNOUS CLOAK OF BEARSKIN CLOTH
1867 PETERSON

(FITS 10" MANNIKIN DOLLS)

In this department, which we call "How To Make One's Own Dresses", we give, every month, a pattern for a cloak, dress, child's costume, or some other garment, accompanied by a diagram by which the article may be cut out, by any housewife, without the aid of a mantuamaker.

The diagrams are, of course, in miniature; but the true size, for a person of ordinary height, is always marked on the different parts, so that it can easily be enlarged, as we have often explained before.

For this month we give a winter cloak for a lady, in a style very fashionable, at present, in Paris. It is a Burnous of bearskin cloth, bordered with silk binding turned over the edge; this garment is closed in front by six buttons.

The sleeve begins on the shoulder, and is afterward entirely detached from the Burnous.

Pointed collar, opening two inches in front at the neck and forming a hood, behind, from the shoulder.

* *

AUTHOR'S NOTE:

BURNOUS OF BEARSKIN CLOTH

Sew back seams together. Sew sleeve C-D to front P-Q. Sew sleeve E-F to back N-O all the way down to the narrow curve.

Now sew the back point M to the front point Q-R, fitting it into the armhole. Bring J to G and stitch to H for shoulder seams, thus forming the elbow of the sleeve. Sew the side seams. Sew N-M to J-K2 and B-C to K1-K2 to form underarm seam.

This done, trim edges with braid or binding of choice. Then tack B-K and A, the two pointed ends of the sleeve, together and sew a tassel which weights the sleeve down and gives the appearance shown in the drawing.

Line all if you wish; it will give the cloak a professional touch and a much nicer appearance.

HOOD

The "X" on the pattern marks the front of the hood. The facings form two hollow pleats behind, indicated by V1 and V2.

Sew back seams together. Catch V, V1, and V2 together to form a pleat. Now sew the top seam to form the hood. Line and edge hood all around with braid or choice of trim. Sew hood to cloak neckline at X's. Fold the hood up in back and let hood hang down on cloak with a tassel sewn at W.

Sew a cord and tassels at each side of hood at point Y where pleats were made. Close front of cloak with tiny buttons; small white pearl buttons may be covered in self material.

* *

BURNOUS CLOAK OF BEARSKIN CLOTH

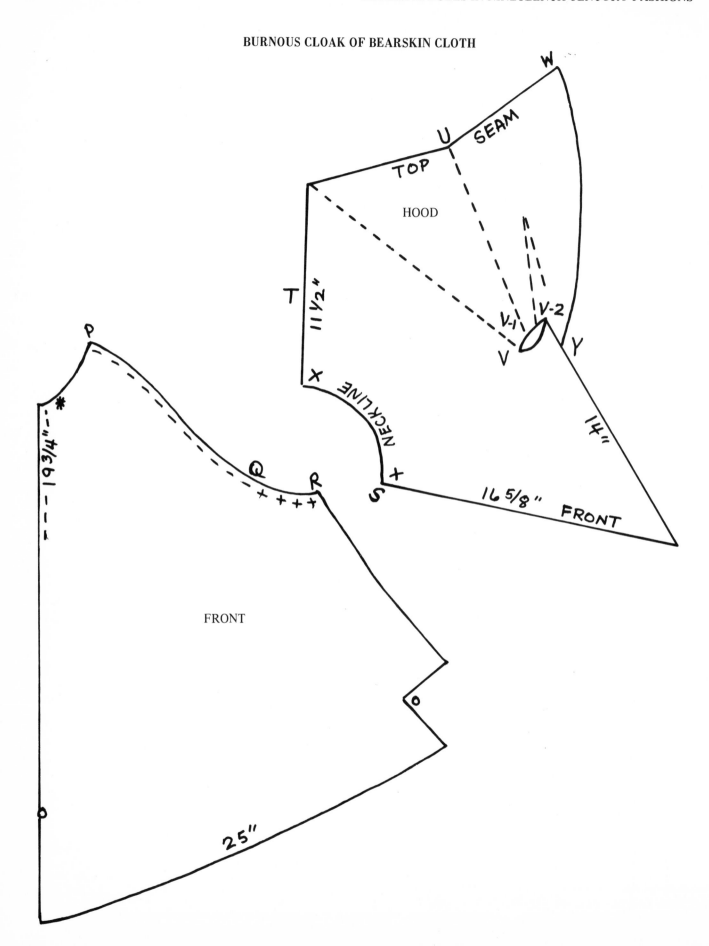

BURNOUS CLOAK OF BEARSKIN CLOTH

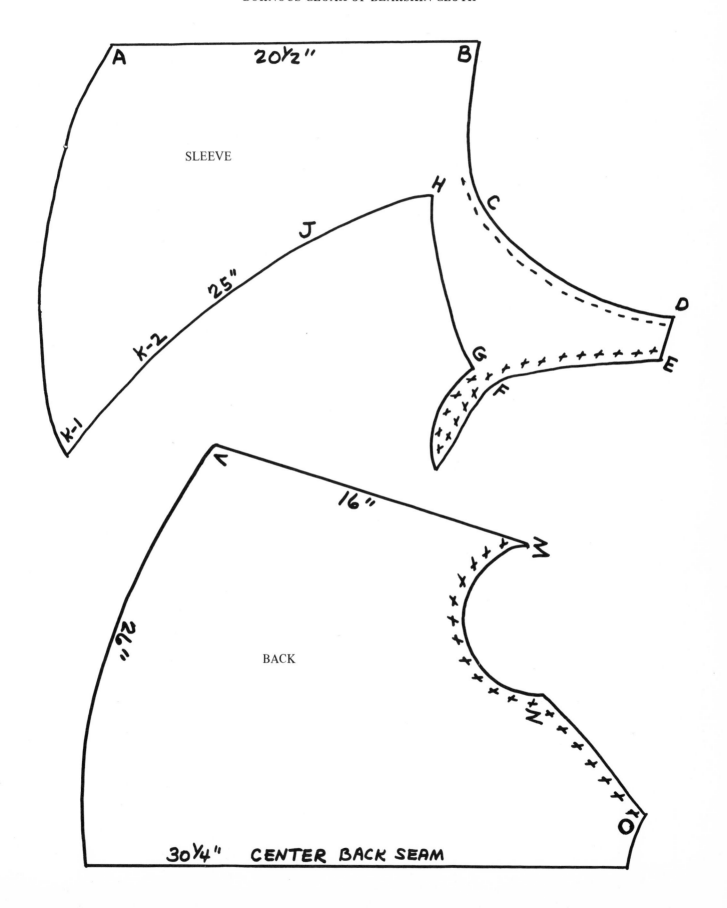

1865 Godey

LATEST STYLE OF ROBE.

(From the celebrated establishment of Messrs. A. T. Stewart & Co., *of New York.)*

Robe and palet't of *toile de lin*, a very pretty wash material. The color is a delicate buff, with the pattern in black. White straw hat, trimmed with buff ribbon, black velvet, and buff feathers.

1865 Godey

LATEST STYLE OF ROBE.

(From the celebrated establishment of Messrs. A. T. Stewart & Co., *of New York.)*

Robe with Zouave jacket and rotonde of a light shade of cuir-color *toile de lin*, printed in black to resemble braiding.

1865 Godey

CASHMERE MORNING DRESS.

(From the celebrated establishment of Messrs. A. T. STEWART & Co., *of New York.)*

This robe is also made with a yoke at the back, and has the skirt set on in heavy box plaits.   It is of a brilliant Solferino
cashmere, with the richest of Persian borders.   The graduated piece up the front and the yoke are of black.

1865 Godey

SPRING SUIT.

Black silk dress. Pearl-colored paletot, trimmed with strips of black velvet. The belt is of black velvet, with jet buckle. Black straw hat, trimmed with black velvet and a purple plume.

1865 Godey

LATEST STYLE OF ROBE.

(From the celebrated establishment of Messrs. A. T. Stewart & Co., *of New York.)*

Cashmere robe of Humboldt purple, with deep bordering of black, ornamented with a narrow border in very rich Persian
designs. It is made with a pointed yoke at the back.

1865 Godey

LA FOLIE PALETOT.

This new spring wrap is made of black silk, and trimmed with quilled ribbon and fringe. Full sized patterns of it can be furnished by our Fashion editress.

1865 Godey

MORNING DRESS.

(*From the celebrated establishment of* Messrs. A. T. STEWART & Co., *of New York.*)

Lavender-colored cashmere robe, with rich bordering of violine purple and black. The back is laid in heavy box plaits, **and** sewed on to a pointed yoke.

1865 Godey

SCENES ON THE ICE.

1865 Godey

DINNER-DRESS FOR A YOUNG LADY.
(Front, Side, and Back view.)

It is worn over a guimpe of tucked French muslin.   This corsage is very suitable for velvet.

Dress of Eugenie blue gros grain, trimmed with black velvet and jet drop buttons.

1865 Godey

COATEE EVENING DRESS.

Coatee evening dress, made of white tarletane, trimmed with puffs of the same. The coatee is lined with blue silk, and trimmed with blue ribbon.

1865 Godey

NOVELTIES FOR FEBRUARY.

1865 Godey

1867 Peterson

BONNETS.

NEW STYLES OF DRESSING HAIR.

1867 Peterson

LOW-NECKED BODICES.

WALKING DRESS

BRETON PALETOT FOR HOUSE

COLLAR AND CUFF.

1867 Peterson

FLANNEL JACKET.

WINTER PALETOTS.

DINNER DRESS.

1867 Peterson

PEPLUM AND BODY.

EVENING DRESS

COLLAR AND CUFF.

LACE BODY.

1867 Peterson

CAP.

BODICE.

COLLAR AND CUFF.

CAPE.

EVENING DRESS.

1867 Peterson

YOUNG LADY'S HAT.

CAP.

PEPLUM

YOUNG LADY'S BONNET.

CARRIAGE DRESS.

VELVET BODY.

1867 Peterson

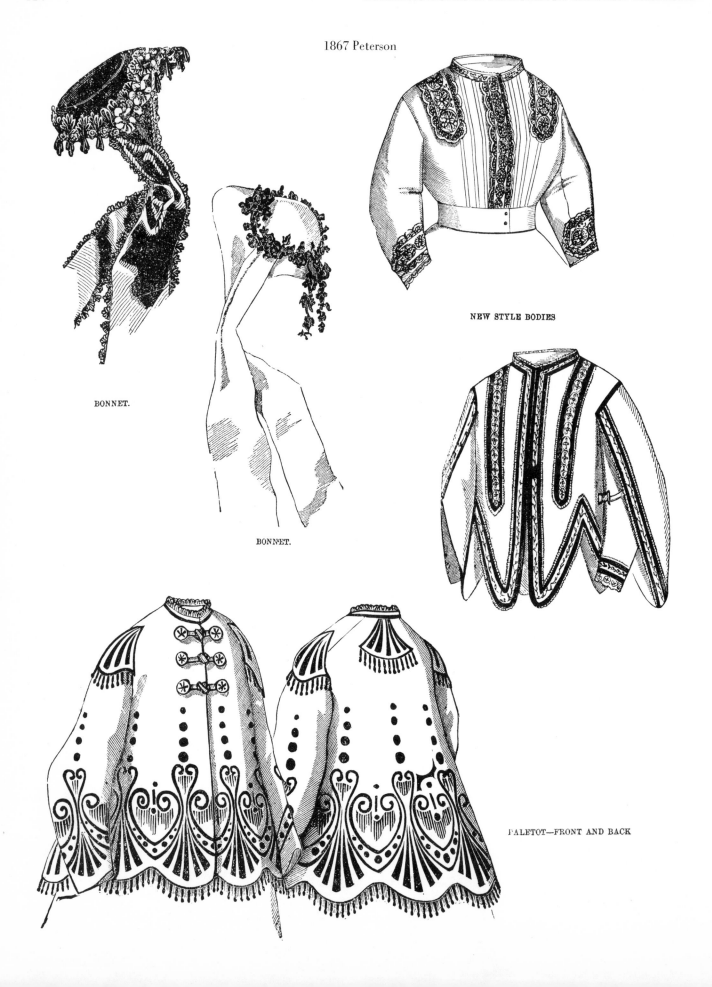

BONNET.

BONNET.

NEW STYLE BODIES

PALETOT—FRONT AND BACK

1867 Peterson

COLLAR, AND SLEEVE.

COLLAR AND CUFF.

BONNETS,

NEW STYLE PARTY DRESS.

1867 Peterson

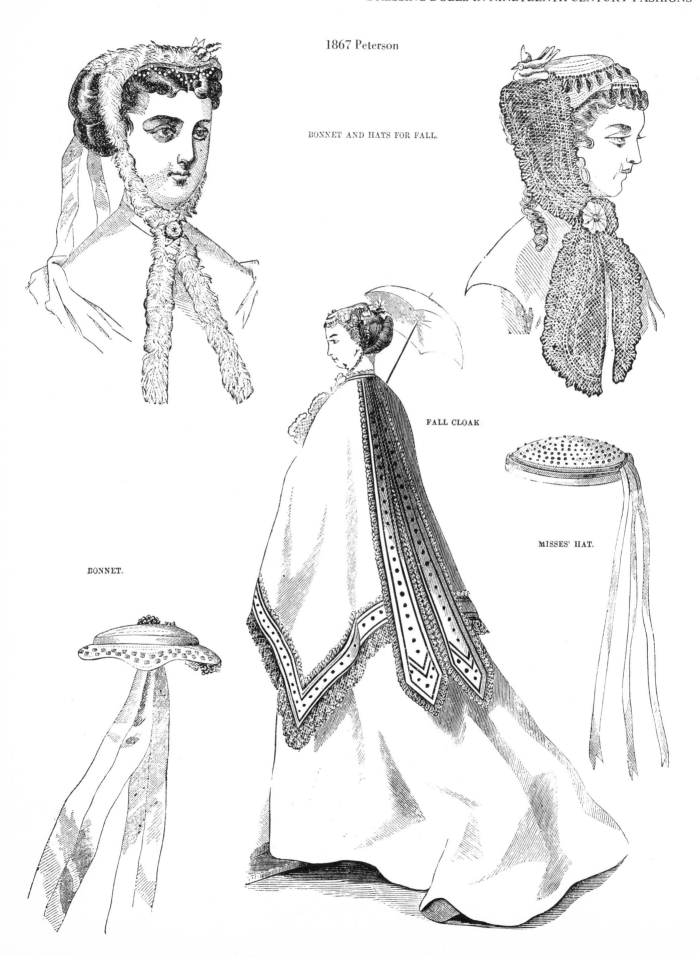

BONNET AND HATS FOR FALL.

FALL CLOAK

MISSES' HAT.

BONNET.

1867 Peterson

BONNET

FALL PALETOT: BACK AND FRONT

CARRIAGE DRESS

WINTER COAT: FRONT AND BACK.

VELVET COAT: FRONT AND BACK.

1867 Peterson

HEAD-DRESSES: BONNET AND HAT.

PART III

* * * * * * * * * * * * * * * * * * *
AUTHOR'S NOTE:

THE 1870s

The 1870s was a very elegant decade; styles featured many fanciful trims and a wide array of colors which are described, often poetically, in the old magazines.

A number of styles of petticoats are shown with diagrams and drawings which should aid immensely in fashioning undergarments for dolls.

With the great selection of materials described there should be no problem in sewing an authentic wardrobe for a doll. Many of these materials, so popular in the 1870s, can easily be substituted from the vast collection of fabrics in department stores and shops today.

* * * * * * * * * * * * * * * * * * *

JANUARY 1870 PETERSON

The Antique red which was so fashionable last year under the name of "Sultane", is just as popular this season; then there is the "dust" color, and the elderberry and grayish-purple, and mostly for out-of-door costume, the warm maroons and the peacock, together with a pale aster-of-roses, shading toward lilac rather than pink; a brilliant coral; Regina, which is darker than mauve; and Absinthe, the faintest tint of blue on white, a marvelously beautiful color, that seems green by gaslight.

Lace, both black and white, is very much used; and velvet never entered more largely into the toilet than it does this year.

Flounces and quillings are in greater vogue than ever, without causing any prejudice to cross strips and rouleaux; all this is mixed together upon modern dresses, and fringes and fancy braids are added besides.

Velvet, in plain bands, or in quillings, as a heading to flounces and flutings, looks best for trimming dresses of woolen material.

The round waists, with sashes, etc., though still worn, are giving place to bodices cut with points, both back and front. For any but a very slim figure, this is much the most becoming style.

The sacques, mantles, etc., are innumerable in styles this winter. If the sacque or jacket is very short and loose, it is cut up the back to fit easily over the panniers which are still worn. If it is only moderately long, it is cut more in the style of the old-fashioned basque; but if it is made longer still, it falls to the trimming of the under-skirt, and is looped up at the sides or back with bows.

By the side of these tight-fitting casaques, one sees redingotes, and loose paletots with revers like men's coats; but perhaps, the newest mantle of the season is the circular, in the Metternick style. The present Metternick is ample at the back, and would be loose if it were not fastened at the waist by a large bow of the material; at the sides it forms great wings, covering the arms in shape of sleeves, while under these wings,

the fronts are tight-fitting as a casaque, or rather a large waistcoat. The mantle is made of velvet or cashmere, lined with silk, or of duite cloth. In velvet it is trimmed with lace and handsome knotted fringe. The bow is also of velvet; if the circular is of cashmere or of cloth, the ornament placed upon it is of cross strips of satin, or else of plain strips of velvet, material as the cross strips.

Bonnets are quite high in front, but otherwise may be made and trimmed in any style that pleases the fancy. The new bonnets are mere diadems of velvet and flowers; there are not even strings, a scarf of gauze or lace takes their place; this veil goes round the chin, and is wrapped round the neck. A great many gold ornaments are seen upon the bonnets, as also upon all fancy mantles. For instance, a dressy bonnet is entirely made of black lace, in front a lace bow is fastened by a gold brooch, a black feather droops at the side. A scarf veil of black lace, brightened up by an edging of gold braid on either side, goes round the face and neck, and is fastened at the side with a gold brooch.

Long dresses, even when looped up, are rarely worn. Ladies have come to the very just conclusion that it is impossible to loop up gracefully the train of the dress. For walking, the costume must be short, made expressly to favor the free motion of the feet, and give the wearer an easy and graceful carriage. Long dresses, however, will continue to be worn indoors, especially at evening parties and grand dinners.

In new trimmings velvet is the material most used; grosgrain is the second choice; satin has fallen somewhat into disfavor. Bands of bias velvet, cut from the piece in varied widths from two inches to a quarter of a yard, are placed straight around skirts, the narrow bands as headings to flounces, wider ones in conjunction with ruches, lace, or fringe. Velvet of the same shade of the dress, is preferable, though black and contrasting colors are used. Ribbon velvet, both wide and narrow, fills the space between flounces. Grosgrain is seen as bias bands piped with satin, or notched with saw-teeth, or edged with passementerie or fringe; also as puffs, quillings, and flounces. Satin is most used in thick cable cords, in facings, and narrow pipings. Straight flounces in large plaits, all turned one way, are seen in profusion on silk and woolen dresses, but few box-plaits are made. Gathered flounces, hitherto thought unsuitable for thick materials are found even on velvet garments, a scant velvet, full piped with satin and faille being prettier than one would imagine.

The new passementerie or crocheted gimp in lace patterns of points and scallops, forms a beautiful edging. Thick, oval ornaments, like elongated buttons and shoulder-knots, or frogs of passementerie, add a dressy appearance to plain cloth suits. Large buttons of satin and velvet rings and crocheted centers are placed in double rows down the fronts of redingotes, and fastened by double loops of thick cord. Chenille fringe is on many of the new suits; also bouillion fringe of thick cable cord, and a heavy fringe of detached tassels. The appropriate trimmings for cloth and woolen materials are velvet, grosgrain, and fringe; for silks, flounces of the same with velvet bands; for velvet, grosfaille facings, satin pipings, passementerie, and lace.

The Empress Jacket is the newest thing in Paris. It is short, wide, and cut with four large basques, which are bordered with Venetian point sewn on plain. The guipure is carried up the back in a point, and the whole is embellished at the edge with narrow gold braid.

Black Velvet Sacques are the style this winter. They are made long, so as to dispense with the tunic, and are to be worn over silk petticoats, for in this way there can be great variety in the toilet, as the petticoat can be easily changed.

FEBRUARY 1870 PETERSON

The Watteau Style continues to reign; paniers at the back, skirts looped up at the sides, and richly trimmed petticoats, are still as popular as last winter. Some of the sleeves of these dresses are of the coat shape, with deep cuffs, others loose, of the old pagoda shape, over a close sleeve.

Overskirts are more worn than ever. The most graceful style for upperskirts, with apron fronts is to make them as long as the underskirt, and drape them in deep plaits on the hips, making them only short enough to show the trimming of the underskirt beneath. Scallops, or castellated points, or else flat bands, trim upper skirts better than frills that rumple easily.

The most fashionable costumes are made with a tunic, forming at once a bodice and mantle. Pointed waists are becoming more and more popular, and for any, save the slightest figures, they are indefinitely the most becoming, though much more difficult to fit nicely than the round waist. All skirts are draped; for ball dresses a thin over-dress is always draped over a silk, or over a satin, which is much more lustrous.

The newest combinations of colors is light-blue worn with dark violet or amethyst color.

All mantles and dresses are made so very high, that great changes have, in consequence, taken place in lingerie. Instead of plain collars turned down, one now wears small standing up collars, or else, what is infinitely more becoming, ruches of fine muslin, tulle, or lace round the neck. For demi-toilet, finely gauffered ruches of clear muslin, simply trimmed or edged with a narrow strip of tulle, have a charming effect; for more elegant sets we see ruches entirely of Valenciennes or Mechlin lace. It is only with bodices open in the shape of a heart that linen collars, with large turned-down revers are worn.

In the evening, there are still fichus and pelerines of tulle and lace, with satin trimmings. With demi-long sleeves, open to the elbow, one wears ruffles of lace, which are extremely becoming, and give much grace to the toilet.

The newest and most coquettish form of bonnet is that called "bebe" or "Infates". It has a small, soft foundation, a tiny curtain at the back and a high coronet in front. All round

the bonent some grosgrain ribbon is twisted. Sometimes the curtain is replaced by a bow of ribbons, as, obviously, a desire to return to curtains is not conspicuous.

Bows are now universally worn on the head; no lady appears to fancy that her toilet is complete without one. They are made in all colors, and to match the dress; but black velvet bows are usually selected by those of simple taste, and exceedingly well do they assimilate with every toilet.

The hair is now worn so low at the back that nets are again in fashionable trend. And the variety called "invisable" are once more called into requisition. The bows are made of wide ribbon, and have two loops; they are arranged precisely as Alsatian women wear them. Sometimes they have four loops, and are made of narrow ribbon, but then they are neither so pretty, nor so stylish looking.

The frills made of muslin (they call them "fraises" in Paris) and trimmed with Valenciennes lace, have quite replaced the plain linen collars.

MARCH 1870 PETERSON

The dresses cut in a heart-shape, or square at the neck, gain popularity everyday. The body is quite high at the back and on the shoulder, and as a general rule, not open very wide in front. Then the half-long sleeves, with the wide ruffles at the elbow, are great favorites; dresses made in this way have a much more "dressy" look than with the older style of "high necks" and tight sleeves. Flounces are more worn than ever, and upper skirts looped up, or made open and looped back with graceful knots and bows of ribbon, add very much to the graceful style of dress. To add to the last century appearance of our ladies, lace is also plentifully used on dresses; but it should be put on fully and richly to look well.

We repeat what we have often said before: The rich costumes or dresses we describe may always be copied in less expensive materials. It is the style, not necessarily the material, that you must follow.

Velvet is so rich that it will be used for bows, etc., on dresses during the summer, but, of course, must be put on sparingly, or else it will look too heavy. Fringes, ribbons, and jet will also continue in favor.

A new fan-holder for fastening the fan at the waist - a great relief to partners - has been introduced; also, gloves for evening wear, with four and even six buttons, adorned at the back of the wrist with a bow of colored ribbon. The gloves, too - strangest innovation of all - are colored to match the dress.

APRIL 1870 PETERSON

The new spring goods are exceedingly pretty and fresh looking; the chintzes, percales, and a new cotton material called satin-jeau, which is a little twilled, and very glossy, are usually of white grounds, with green, blue, or violet stripes;

or else with polka dots, or with small flower patterns over them. Some of the prettiest percales are perfectly plain, and of delicate tea, buff, dove, or pearl colors. Lawns and organdies are striped in white or of some delicate shade of color, alternating with strips of a gay chintz pattern.

Mohairs are in stripes and checks of all the pretty spring colors; French summer silks are always beautiful, and vary but little in pattern, the small plaids and narrow stripes being always in fashion; they come in all the most delicate shades of color. The foulards, which have been of such poor quality for so many years, are of much more serviceable texture this year; they are twilled, have light grounds, and are dotted with pretty contrasting colors, as a buff ground with light-blue; maize color with brown; gray with violet, etc., and some have flowers sprinkled over them; others are striped etc. Grenadines are of all colored grounds, with brocaded stripes and flowers.

There are innumerable materials of cotton and silk and wool combinations, with innumerable names attached; but they are usually of the styles described. Black silks are still very high, if of good quality as well as all other good silks of single colors. For very elegant dresses, either as an over-skirt for a short suit, or as a tunic over a train dress, crepe de chine is very stylish. This is something like the old-fashioned China crepe, except it is much lighter in texture, and finer, with a less crepe surface. This is of French manufacture, and not Chinese. It has body enough to make a long dress and is usually trimmed with lace, or a narrow moss fringe.

A long dress is never seen on the street now, and a short one is seldom seen in the evening, except on very young girls. There is nothing particularly new in the way of making dresses. For the street, the lower skirt is trimmed with either one deep ruffle or several narrower ones, or with puffings, quillings, etc., as the fancy may dictate. The upper skirt is usually a good deal puffed at the back, draped at the sides, and should always be trimmed to correspond, in some measure, with the underskirt. Even for the street, the dresses will be worn square, or slightly open in front, over a chemisette; and while some cling to the close coat sleeve, others prefer the tight sleeve to just below the elbow, with two or three deep ruffles, or the old-fashioned pagoda sleeve, reaching to the wrist, and very wide.

Sacques, very much draped and puffed made of black silk, come this season to wear over dresses of all colors; but an article of the same kind can be made of the color of the underskirt, and thus form a complete costume. Very short jackets, slit up the back and under the arms, so as to give room for the panniers, and with long, wide flowing sleeves, will also be worn on the street.

Long dresses for the house are also very much trimmed; ruffles, flounces, and bows of ribbon, are seen everywhere; the puffed tunic still keeps its place; square and heart-shaped bodices are much the most fashionable. Lace is very much employed in all trimmings.

Since the open bodices have been worn, more attention has been paid to linen; and lace, its appropriate trimming, is now universally used for ladies collars, cuffs, and frills. The chem-

isette a coeur, square, and the collar, Henri 11, are very pretty, but the latter is most becoming to persons with long necks. After all, the most important thing to be observed in dress is whether a particular style, shape, or color suits the wearer's age, figure, height, or complexion. The present fashions are most varied, and every woman ought to be able to discover the one most suited to improve instead of to uglify appearance. There is a greater art in dressing well than many would suppose; thus the short costume often looks ungraceful, not because it fits badly, but from the simple reason that the under-skirts have not received proper attention.

Only the smallest kind of crinoline or hoop is worn; just enough to make a person walk comfortably, if the dress be either long or short; the hoops should in no instance meet in front, either at the top or bottom.

The new bonnets still retain the winter's shape, very small at the back, and very high in front. Feathers are a great deal used, but as the season advances, they will give way to long sprays of flowers.

Among New Materials are the Beaver Brand, black Mohair, and the Buffalo Brand, and Black Alpaca. They are probably the best things imported. They combine elegance and cheapness in an unrivaled degree, and will outwear any other articles in the same line of goods. To a great extent they will supersede black silk. The other materials for spring dresses are much as usual.

MAY 1870 PETERSON

Light Green Shades are very fashionable this season. The newest are the Water of the Nile green, almond-green, and Colibri green, the latter of great brilliancy, with sparkling gold yellow lights; in velvet or satin it calls to mind the bright plumage of certain birds of the West Indies.

Spring and Summer Dresses this year will be, to a great extent, made of two materials, or of two tints, or even sometimes of two colors. In the latter case, beware of glaring contrasts of unharmonizing shades; the mixture of colors has always been a stumbling block in the female toilet, and it is, perhaps, for that reason that one hears it said so often of several people that they are never so well dressed as when they are in mourning, better a hundred times in uniformity than badly matched colors, and even plain black than too great a variety of tints. A theory which it is well not to lose sight of, and which indeed, is vary simple, is this: There should never be more than two positive colors in a lady's toilet; black and white are not reckoned as such. Both the colors must harmonize well together, of course; if one is neutral, the other must be well defined; if one is dark, the other must possess a certain brightness. This year in toilettes of two shades, the underskirt and mantle will be made of one color, the dress of another. The flounces, of the same material as that part of the dress of which they form the trimming, will be edged with cross-strips or pipings of the other color. This toilet will not form the general rule, at least as great a number will be made of one tint, or of two shades of one color.

Among the new importations for dress goods, pongees are the most desirable; they are cool, glossy, and most serviceable, many of them washing admirably; for a short suit nothing can be more stylish than a gray or buff pongee, the underskirt ruffled, and either trimmed in the same color or with black; or, if for a young person, with crimson silk; or, what is equally stylish, a black silk underskirt, with the upper one and waist of yellow pongee, prettily draped. The old-fashioned mousseline delaine is also being revived; this is particularly appropriate for draped dresses, as it falls so softly, and is inexpensive. Pongee costs one dollar and twenty-five cents per yard. Unbleached linens are also much sought after for summer dress; these are in shades of yellow and gray, and cost one dollar per yard. Organdies and white muslins always are popular, except for the sea-shore, where they are of but little use. A new way of using white muslin is very charming, and an old blue, green, pink, or mauve silk dress, may be made to look quite new by its use. Large flounces, or pleatings of white muslin, edged with a plain "footing", or with an excellent imitation of Valenciennes, are put on the front of the skirt, and a long tunic, trimmed in the same way, falls like a court train over the skirt and is looped up with bows of black velvet or with ribbon of the color of the dress. Sometimes these muslin flounces are put on under silk ones, reaching only a few inches below the knee.

The fashion of wearing two skirts may be turned to good account, however, by those who possess a number of light-colored dresses of thin material; since by cutting the gored skirts shorter they can be made fuller at the waist, and the piece taken off the top will form a trimming for the front of the underskirt. A tunic or train open in front, displaying the underskirt very long, and disposed in short puffs, in panier at the back, with a low or square bodice, will form a toilet at once fashionable and effective. The upper dress may be of the same color as the under one, but always of a darker shade.

Pointed waists are obtaining favor, not only because they are new (which is often the recommendation to an American woman), but because they are so very becoming to all but very slender figures; these latter look better in waistbands. Basques of various shapes are also gaining ground; these are particularly desirable for street costume when a jacket or sacque are not worn.

JUNE 1870 PETERSON

A few new changes have taken place in the style of skirts, etc., first indication of this is the suppression of the extremely puffed skirt; second, by the larger introduction of the velvet revers in the body, occasionally accompanied by vests; and thirdly, the adoption of the collarette Medicis for the more elegant visiting dresses. It would appear moreover, that lace is about to enter largely into the trimming of all silk and satin robes; and there is a growing indication of the underskirt, which is now so elaborately trimmed, being worn without any trimming at all. The waistband, too, is on the eye of being

suppressed and to compensate for its abandonment, corsages will be pointed at the waist in front or be made with broad square, or rounded basques, or with a series of small vandykes or scallops. At the same time that the trimming of the underskirts of walking dresses show signs of being abandoned, the same skirts of evening dresses are being ornamented with flounces, bands, rouleaux, and ruches up to the very waist. Sleeves are being worn loose at the ends, and occasionally pointed in shape.

The Bonnets are, many of them, faithful copies of those worn during Louis XVI's reign, and possess a certain grace peculiarly their own. First in the list there is the "Charlotte Corday" bonnet, made of black tulle and black lace and is precisely the same shape as the celebrated cap of the beautiful Charlotte. It towers high at the top of the head and has a gathering or fullness of black lace over the forehead. A large, black velvet bow ornaments the bonnets, and either a tuft of cerise roses is fastened at the side, or what is more poetical, a branch of the chestnut tree in full bloom. The strings are black velvet.

Hats are mostly worn high, or the trimming is disposed in such a manner as to make them appear so. Many of them are turned up on the left side and have a stylish and at the same time jaunty look. Gauze and China crepe are both much used to trim hats; and black lace appears on nearly all. A few well-trimmed Leghorn hats have appeared for country wear and croquet; but they are most unbecoming; except on children, though we acknowledge very useful. The Chinese hat protects the face equally well, and is more becoming; it has no crown, only a slight elevation in the center, and is usually trimmed with only a knot of ribbon or velvet, though a small bunch of flowers sometimes put on top.

JULY 1870 PETERSON

The threatened change of short to long skirts for street dresses will be heard of with regret by all sensible people; that they are more elegant no one will deny, though for young girls, the short skirts, puffed and bowed in a moderate degree, are very jaunty. As yet none of the out-of-door dresses received from Paris are made with train skirts; but they are longer than they were last year; touching the ground at the back, and proportionally long all round. Some of these are made with a short court-train over the very much trimmed petticoat; for the street this train is looped up in a graceful manner, and let down for the house. Underskirts or petticoats are most elaborately trimmed with ruffles, puffs, pleats, etc., and black lace and fringe are also very much used, as well as bows and loops of ribbon. Some of the newest French dresses have points both back and front; some a point only at the back, with a waistband and bow in front; and others with a point in front, with a waistband (reaching from the side seams) and a bow at the back. Dresses of fine, unbleached linen are trimmed with flounces and ruffles of the white embroidery; and edging and insertion of unbleached thread. Some of these linens can be bought as low as twenty five cents a yard, but they are coarse, and they vary in price from that up to two dollars per yard.

White muslin dresses are trimmed with ruffles and knots of ribbon, though some are more elaborate, and are ornamented with Valenciennes lace, and very expensive. Figured organdies are sometimes plain, but most frequently ruffled with either stripes of the same, or with white organdy.

Straw Bonnets of an entirely different shape from those worn during the winter are worn; they fit on the back of the head over the braids, and come close to the hair in front. They are usually trimmed with a narrow pleating of ribbon or tulle on the inside, and are much ornamented with flowers and gauze, or crepe de chine.

AUGUST 1870 PETERSON

Soft shades, such as chamois, fawn, vapor, putty, buff-color, and all the series of gray tints, are very fashionable this summer, and often they are shot or striped with white. Besides foulards, organdies, and printed muslins, one sees but few figured materials; the pretty goat's-hair and fancy wool and silk materials of which demi-toilet walking costumes are made, are for the most part, self-colored, shot, or striped; it is the same with silks, glace silks, faille, or grosgrain.

The loose Paletots, which have been much worn during the earlier summer, are now beginning to be exchanged for tight-fitting casaques, forming bodices and double-skirt, and so useful in summer. One also sees mantelets, but they also are fastened to the waist by a large sash, which also makes them resemble casaques.

Mantles, like dresses, open in front, in the shape of a heart or point. Sleeves for both the one and the other, are made at pleasure, tight or streaming, with creves in the Henry III style, to the pagoda sleeves, or the Oriental sleeves, slit open from the elbow, they are made in all manner of fashions.

White Bodices are much gone out of fashion; they are now exchanged for pretty chemisettes to accompany low dresses, or those that are open in front. These chemisettes, embroidered and trimmed with lace, are a luxury in good taste. For sometime past, ruches of tulle clear muslin or lace, have taken the place of plain collars. This is extremely becoming. Another pretty fashion is that of muslin fichus, trimmed with embroidery and Valenciennes lace, worn with low dresses. These are the real coquettish fichu menteurs of the marchionesses of last century. It is a fashion very becoming to thin ladies. While recommending to them this fichu, we would warn them against the bodices cut low and square in front; this style of bodice has the effect of showing the chest narrower; and is suitable only to rather stout ladies. When one has a perfectly good figure, one may wear anything one chooses; but, when one carries rather too far either the excess of thinness or the excess of embonpoint, there are certain details which it is well to observe.

To ladies gifted with embonpoint, we recommend dark materials, long waists, but few flounces, and those placed very low down, the train-shaped tunic rather than the double skirt, no puff, at the utmost a wide sash, the loops of which puff out the tournure a little behind.

Flounces, with fluted headings put on upward, are also frequently seen upon the new toilettes. Sometimes three or four of these flutings are put on above one flounce. At other times small, fluted flounces are put on under a deeper flounce; in fact, all possible combinations are adopted, and the great art of seamstresses seem to be to vary these combinations as much as possible.

As for Coiffures, the hair now descends on the neck in curls, or is merely waved and enclosed in an invisible net. For neglige, waged and falling chignons are the latest novelty; these will be still prettier with the summer hats, for which they appear to be an indispensable complement. The chignons standing off from the neck, which were still in favor last summer, have lost all their vogue.

SEPTEMBER 1870 PETERSON

As a general rule, dresses are not as short, and the boot is not seen as it used to be; skirts, neither short nor training. Just to the ground, and are trimmed at bottom with flounces, ruches, or plaitings; tunics of crepeline or crepe de chine complete charming toilets; they are gracefully draped and confined round the waist by a scarf-sash with a large bow.

Petticoats of black silk, trimmed with many small ruffles, or with one or two deep ones, with an over-skirt, and jacket or paletot of black cashmere, are among the least expensive and most stylish street dresses. Brown cashmere and silk look equally well. We see an inclination to wear for out-of-doors but one skirt, but this is most elaborately trimmed with ruffles or puffs that reach nearly to the waist; then a jacket or paletot is added; no upper-skirt or tunic. We do not know that this style is an improvement, in the way of saving material or labor, and it is certainly not so graceful as the looped-up over-skirt. In fact, all dresses are so elaborately trimmed that the number of yards of silk required are enormous. A letter from Paris says: "when you order a costume without paletot, simply a tunic bodice and all-round skirt, dressmakers decline to undertake it unless they have twenty-two or twenty-three yards of wide silk. This quantity really appears enormous; yet such are the requirements of fashion".

Among new trimmings are ruches, composed of strips of silk material, unraveled so as to form a fringe, up to two-thirds of their width or depth, which varies from three to four inches, placed double these ruches resemble the trimmings of curled feathers worn this winter. They are put on as heading to flounces, or round the edge of tunics and double skirts.

Milliners have made many attempts to increase the size of bonnets, but the coiffures remain so very voluminous that bonnets or hats can find but very little place upon the head. But, by compensation, they are getting higher everyday.

OCTOBER 1870 PETERSON

Straight scarfs are made for all dresses of transparent material, such as Swiss muslins, grenadines, etc. The fashion, however, is still exceptional and almost entirely confined to Paris. The arrangement of the scarf is, indeed, a little theatrical. A few plaits are made on the upper-edge of the scarf in the middle of the back, the scarf is then laid on the high bodice, and is fastened with a pin on each shoulder, after which it is crossed in front, and knotted about half-down the skirt of the dress, looping up the latter a little, so as to make it bouffant. Some knot it higher, and others again tie it under the left arm instead of behind.

Cashmere and very fine merino will be more worn this season thnn usual. The petticoats are usually of silk, either black or of the color of the dress, and the upper skirt and jacket, or tunic, are of cashmere.

Short dresses are still popular; but we are sorry to say that they are now made to touch the ground, and as they are trimmed beyond the knee, they are cut narrower than in the spring. The full trimming looks rich and elegant, but the length of the skirt make it less tidy than when an inch or so shorter. Ladies, however, willingly rid themselves of the train, and it is only exceptionally that it is seen now, even for great ceremonies in the daytime. In the evening, they are the indispensable adjunct of dressy toilets, although round dresses are already made sometimes. All that depends upon taste. The Grande Dame wears the train with ease, and will always prefer it to the short dress, but it requires much practice, and a natural grace which cannot be taught, to look well with the court train.

We must say, however, that brides' dresses are always made train-shaped, the bride not going out on foot, may let her dress trail without uneasiness on that account. So also, the bridesmaids, if they choose, wear either the long or the short dress.

The only thing which cannot be tolerated is the train-shaped dress in the street, whether it trail in the dust, or whether it be gathered up in a heap, it will always appear ungainly. It looks ladylike only when it can be spread out at ease upon a carpet without any dread of stain or dust.

Luxury could not well increase in female toilets; for some years past it has been making too rapid progress, but it seems that it is spreading more, and each day becomes more absorbing.

Materials and trimmings, formerly confined to evening toilets, now appear in full daylight. Even the simplest costumes, that is, those which by their material, pretend to be no more than demi-toilet, have most elaborate patterns and trimmings. Velvet ribbon is profusely used for trimmings on all materials, and one of the newest styles of making deep flounces is to place perpendicular bands of velvet ribbon of any width that suits the taste (it should not be less than one inch in width, however) between the plaitings of the flounces. A very little gold is sometimes used on black trimmings, but it is not in good style to use it too lavishly. Fringes are very much used,

and nothing can be prettier than the little narrow moss-fringe, which is so soft, and can either be used along, or as the heading of a longer fringe. Among the new shades are the olives, maroons, prunes, various wine-colors, blues, grays, etc.

The bonnets made with border, crown, and curtains, are placed so very much in front, that they have no longer the appearance of former bonnets, though they have very nearly their shape. Some of them have a border lowered upon the forehead, then a high crown, the hollow part between the border and crown being filled up by a voluminous trimming of ribbons, ruches, feathers, and flowers.

NOVEMBER 1870 PETERSON

Cashmere is more popular than ever. It is less expensive than silk, falls softly and gracefully in the folds required for the present style of dress, and can be worn on almost any occasion. To make the costume more dressy, the petticoat can be of silk instead of cashmere, and if black, it can be trimmed with a good deal of guipure lace, fringe, or gimp of a wide kind, known as passementerie. Of course, with these expensive trimmings the cashmere suit would cost as much as a silk one. The colors are much less bright than those of former seasons; the old-fashioned plum and prune colors (the former on a purplish cast, the latter on a blue), dark, forest-green, navy-blue, chestnut-brown, slate-grays, etc., are all being revived; these are seen in poplins, merinoes, silks, etc., but in an infinite variety of shades.

Braiding is being revived on dresses, mantles, etc., but a round braid is used in place of the flat braid formerly in vogue, and looks much more like embroidery. Braid of the color of the dress should always be used.

Curious combinations of color are now in use, such as maroon and light-blue, maroon and chestnut, maroon and gray, etc. Petticoats of black velvet are very popular, as they can be worn with almost any costume. We have seen one with a flounce of embroidered foulard silk around the bottom, and worn with a foulard casaque, looped up high on the hips. Black silk petticoats can also be worn with almost any costume. Over these can be worn the long casaque of any color, which can be gracefully looped up at the sides or the back or the short draped overdress, with the loose or tight-fitting sacque. There is a prophecy of a fewer trimmings than formerly on the lower skirt or petticoat, but we have seen no evidence of it yet. Basques of all kinds will be worn, and either with or without belts, as may be desired, and with or without a large bow at the back. The costumes from the gray or brown Scotch shawls are exceedingly nice and useful, only they should be draped by a tasteful hand if they are to look elegant.

For evening dresses the most delicate colors are used; the waists are low in the neck or cut out in a heart-shape in front, with rather wide hanging sleeves. The skirts are much or little trimmed, to suit the taste of the wearer; flounces pinked, or scalloped, and bound; ruches made of silk raveled; flounces of white embroidery on muslin are all used, with in fact, any other mode of trimming that the fancy may dictate.

We give in our plates some of the newest style of basques; they can be made of velvet, beaver-cloth, silk, plush, cashmere, or any other material that may be deemed best.

Sleeves are either of the coat-shape or loose, if the latter, a tight-fitting dress sleeve should be worn underneath. The mantle called Infante is destined to be a great success. It consists of two capes, which are square in front. At the back it has a sort of long, flat plait, which descends midway, and is fastened to the waistband. The form is well suited to a tall, slight figure.

The Infante is made of black China crepe, ornamented with a very fine round braid that has all the effect of embroidery. It is edged with handsome black blonde which may be replaced either by a fringe, with a netted heading or by guipure. The Infante mantle is also made of the same material as the dress.

We have seen it completing a gray cashmere costume. The petticoat which was extremely novel, was of gray silk, trimmed with cross-bands of cashmere to the waist. Each band was edged with a gray worsted Tom Thumb fringe. The cashmere tunic that opened in front, was bordered with a crossband of gray silk, edged with the tiny ball-fringe. It was looped up at the back with a single pouf. The Infante mantle had no other trimming than a silk cross-band with worsted ball fringe. The effect was charming.

All bonnets tend to the gipsy shape, of what is called the "Marie Antoinette Gipsy". These have suitable crowns, and caps, and strings tying under the chin.

DECEMBER 1870 PETERSON

In colors, the new dark, almost invisable greens, blues, browns, and plum-colors, are very popular; they are serviceable, and a change from the black so long worn. The newest color is a rich red, which is called Prussian Crimson.

Underskirts for short dresses touch the floor, except just in front, a pretty but untidy fashion, really less clearly than a longer skirt, where the facing (which can be renewed) takes the soil. These underskirts are between three and one-half yards and three and three-quarters yards wide; the front width is but slightly gored, the side width much gored, and the two back widths not gored at all, but gathered as full as possible. The trimming of these skirts may, of course, suit the taste of the wearer.

The upperskirt is usually puffed upon the hips, and at the back, and falls low on the underskirt behind. But the modes of looping a skirt are as varied as the styles of trimming or of making the waist. All styles are becoming and fashionable, and a lady may appear with or without crinoline, with a long, tight-fitting or half-fitting basque, or a loose, short jacket, with trimming of flounces, or ruffles, or lace, or fringe; with a body with basques; in short, so the general form of the costume is preserved, the details may be what one pleases.

The basque is so much newer than the sash and belt so long worn, that it is very popular; the basque may be either long or short, open at the sides, or the back, or not at all.

Some of the newest dresses have points in front with a bow of the dress material at the back; others have a long, soft point at the back, with a belt going from the seams under the arms, and fastened with a bow in front.

Fringe is very much used, especially on upperskirts; for cashmere this is very pretty and suitable, giving a richness to the dress, which makes it rival a silk costume. We must state, however, that handsome silk fringe is expensive.

Paletots, Casaques, etc., follow the style of the skirts. They must be cut with a good deal of spring to fall easily over the large puffed skirts now worn; but there is otherwise no artistic rule, anyone may follow her own fancy as to wearing her paletot tight or half-loose, having it much or plainly trimmed, with tight or loose sleeves, etc.

Bonnets have decidedly changed since last spring, the gipsy (as we have before stated) being now the newest and most popular shape. These bonnets have decided fronts, which are not becoming to all faces, and they require that the front hair should be rolled up from the face, or a good deal frizzed, in order to fill up the space between the forehead and top of the bonnet. Some persons, who do not like their hair in either of these styles, fill up the open space with a quilling of blonde lace. Satin will not be much worn; but velvet will take its place. Two or three shades of the same color will be worn in one bonnet with tips of feathers shaded to correspond, and a large flower. Black velvet bonnets are trimmed with white plumes, white lace, or pippings of white satin.

Applique Embroidery, done by hand, will be much worn. This elegant trimming may be used for many purposes. Jackets of black cloth, or cashmere, embroidered in many colors, are both elegant and useful. This embroidery has a charming effect on Opera Cloaks, mourning dresses, and aprons.

Some original and beautiful muffs and collars have recently been introduced; they are made of feathers from the black-cock, pheasant, peacock, and various fancy birds. These muffs are bright and warm.

The newest things, in the way of fancy articles, are called "floral jewels". They consist of brooches, earrings, and other trinkets, in endless varieties of shape and color. The floral designs are original and very graceful. It is the thing to wear these novel ornaments to match in color with the costume worn with them.

BUTTERFLY

EMBROIDERY DESIGNS FROM 1870 PETERSON

INSERTION EDGING

END OF CRAVAT

EDGING

INSERTION IN EMBROIDERY

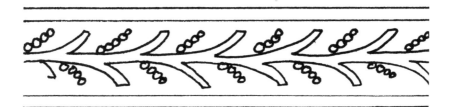

EMBROIDERY INSERTION

BUTTON-HOLE EDGE FOR FLANNEL

EMBROIDERY DESIGNS FROM 1870 PETERSON

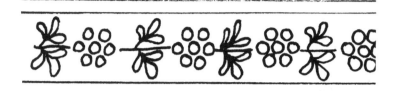

DESIGN INSERTION

TRIMMING OF BRAID IN PIQUE

EDGING

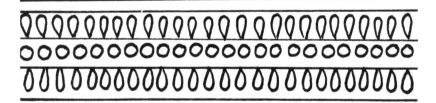

EDGING

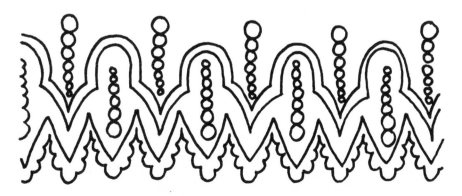

SILK EMBROIDERY ON FLANNEL

MARCH 1870 PETERSON LOW BODICE AND PANNIER TUNIC
(FITS 10" MANNIKIN DOLLS)

This pattern is one of the latest novelties from Paris, and can be made up in a variety of styles in white tarletan, with satin braces of some bright color, and edged with blonde in silk, with velvet braces; or again, in velvet, with lace braces. In one and all these materials it looks remarkably well. It is, of course, for evening wear.

We give a diagram, from which to cut it out. It consists of five pieces - three for the bodice and two for the tunic. The front and back and one brace form the pattern of the bodice; four braces will be required, as there are two in front and two at the back; but, as all four are cut exactly the same, only one has been given. The small holes that mark the darts show the front of the bodice; the position of the braces is marked in a similar manner on both the front and back. The braces may be either cut in one piece for each back and front, or joined on the shoulder, as most convenient. The two pieces for the tunic now remain. The front is the smaller one; it turns back with a revers, the two notches indicate how it is to be joined to the corresponding two notches on the panier. The edge of the side of the panier is to be gathered and sewn to the side of the front. The back is to be bunched up accord-

ing to the illustration, and a short, wide sash added over it. Ruches, plaited ribbon, lace, feathers, and fringe may be used for trimming; the selection to be ruled by the material used.

* * * * * * * * * * * * * * * * * * * *

AUTHOR'S NOTE:

Cut each pattern piece from fabric and lining. Sew pieces 4 and 2 front and back side seams, matching notes. Sew shoulder seams. Gather at neckline and waistline, front and back, allowing for back closing, to fit doll. Sew narrow ruches to front and back of bodice as shown in drawing. Line all. Sew braces and line, add lace ruching or trim of choice.

Sew tunic front to tunic back matching notches, line all, trim with ruching. Turn revers back as seen in drawing and catch stitch to hold in place. Follow directions for bunching tunic back as shown. Sew tunic to bodice waistline, make a sash of ribbon and bows, trim as seen in drawing. Sew braces on bodice shoulders and tack to front and back center waist. Sew bows to shoulder seams. Use the diagram for "An All-Round Skirt", reducing if necessary, to complete a beautiful evening fashion.

* * * * * * * * * * * * * * * * * * * *

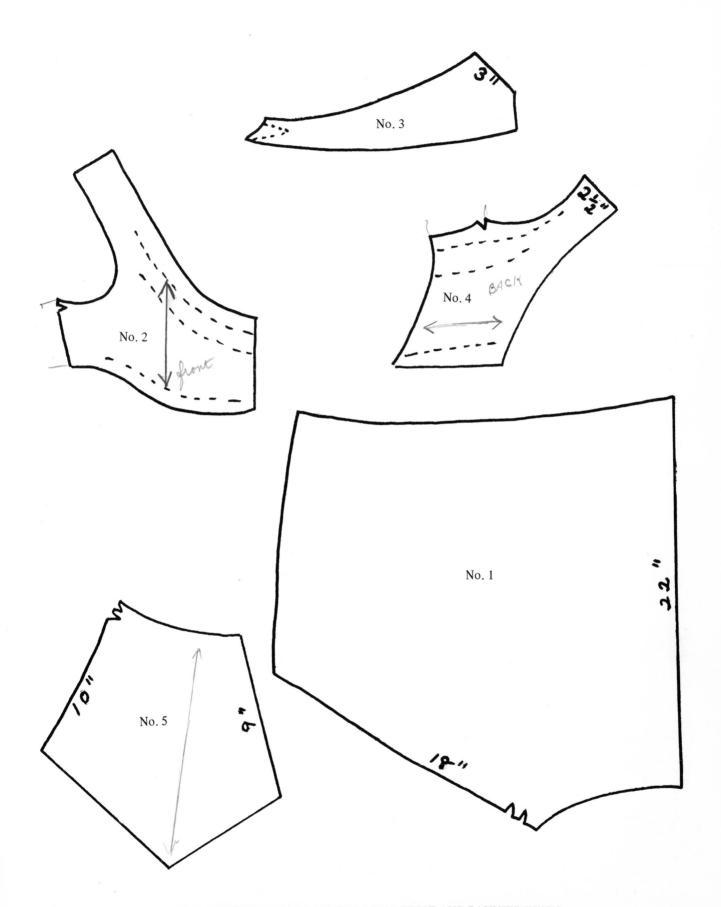

1870 PETERSON DIAGRAM FOR LOW BODICE AND PANNIER TUNIC

THE CHEVALIER CASAQUE APRIL 1870 PETERSON
(FITS 10" MANNIKIN DOLLS)

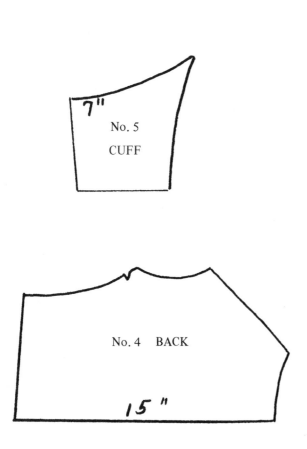

We give here an engraving and diagram of one of the newest and prettiest affairs of the season.

It is called "The Chevalier Casaque", and the pattern consists of five pieces which represent half of the casaque: Front, back, pannier, sleeve, and gauntlet.

Our model is trimmed with lace and ruche. The trimming is laid on the bodice to simulate a square-cut one.

The front joins to the back according to the notches at the edges of the paper. The panier is gathered into the back of the waist; the sides of the panier are likewise gathered, and the sides of the fronts wrap over the panier, and are fastened with either a bow or a gimp ornament. A waistband and short, bunchy sash complete the casaque, which is just the thing for out of door wear in the spring.

* *
AUTHOR'S NOTE:

This is a beautiful style. Use the "All-Round Skirt" pattern, add a pleated flounce and fringe trim or lace. Cut pattern pieces of dress material and lining. Sew pieces 2 and 4 at the waistline. Line all pieces, trim sleeve gauntlet or cuff, sew sleeve seams. Sew shoulder seams; sew side seams matching notches. Trim tunic all round, stitch cuffs to sleeves and sleeves to armholes. Attach tiny snaps to bodice front for closing. Sew tiny buttons on bodice as shown in drawing. Make a small lace collar and tack to neckline. Fashion a belt to fit doll's waist and attach with a small bow. Gather tunic skirt and bunch as described above. Add bows or trims of choice.

* *

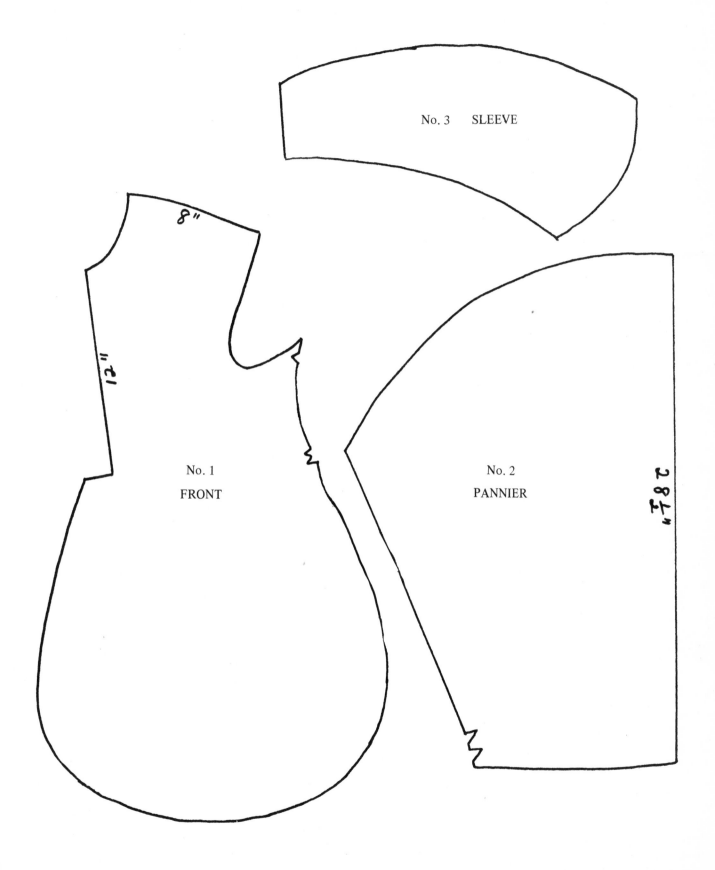

DIAGRAM FOR CHEVALIER CASAQUE APRIL 1870 PETERSON

APRIL 1870 PETERSON

PETTICOATS

Black Silk Underskirt: A very useful underskirt, which may be put on under almost any dress, is represented in this engraving. This underskirt is made of black silk, and is trimmed with a deep puffing, fastened down with a narrow scalloped edge, and a flounce put on with a heading and scalloped on both sides. All scallops are edged with black satin. The shape and style of this underskirt may be copied in a cheaper material, if wished.

Crinoline With Tournure: The latest style of crinoline is shown in an engraving given. This underskirt, or crinoline, as it is so generally called, is made entirely of white horsehair. The tournure is formed of puffs, which are continued at the sides in the lower part. The front is quite plain.

BLACK SILK
UNDERSKIRT

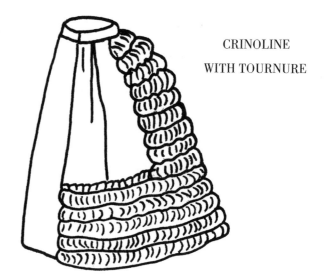

CRINOLINE
WITH TOURNURE

SLEEVES OF 1870 PETERSON

The sleeve we give here is quite plain at the upper part. It is suitable for pique, percales, or muslin dresses. The frills are bound with wash braid on the material, cut bias, and scallops or points may be substituted, or the frills may be made quite plain. The band dividing the frills is bound on both sides, and buttons are dotted on it at intervals.

SASHES OF 1870 PETERSON

As sashes are indispensable, we give three of the prettiest designs we have seen.

The first is of wide, plaid ribbon, combined with black ribbon of velvet; the ends either fringed out, or else a wide, knotted fringe tied in.

The second consists of two colors, or rather any one color, and black combined; heavy silk fringe on the ends. Blue and black, or scarlet and black, worn with pique dresses in fall, always look pretty.

The third is made of black silk or velvet ribbon; the bows are made fan-shaped and box-plaited. It can easily be trimmed and formed from the engraving. Tassels can be made at home out of skeins of black and white sewing-silk. Two skeins of sewing-silk will make a very nice tassel.

No. 1

No. 2

No. 3

NEW MODE OF LOOPING UP A SKIRT
SEPTEMBER 1870 PETERSON

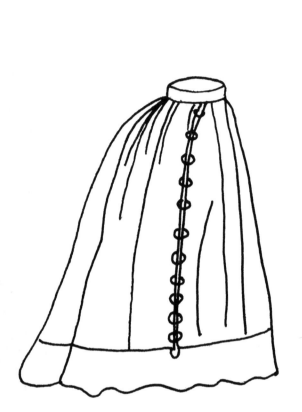

We give two engravings showing a new mode of looping up a skirt. To loop a skirt in the manner seen in these illustrations, sew a number of small rings down each side on the wrong side, and draw through these rings a silk cord on either side, by means of which the skirt is taken up. The rings must be sewn on at intervals of about four inches. One end of the cord is fastened below the lowest circle; the other end is drawn through a slit made in the skirt in front at the waistband on the right-hand side of the skirt; sew on tassels or buttons at the ends of the cord, so as to prevent its sliding back through the slit. This manner of taking up dresses is very suitable for such as have short trains only. If the train of the dress be very long, two other cords must be drawn through two other rows of brass rings in the middle of the back, taking the cords double. All these cords are drawn at the same time through the slit at the side of the skirt, fastening likewise tassels or buttons at the ends. This process is both simple and effective.

1870 PETERSON PETTICOAT FOR SHORT DRESSES
(FITS 10" - 11" CHINA DOLLS)

The skirts of dresses are still made to hang considerably fuller at the back than in front. As lined dresses are not much in vogue, the Parisian modistes have devised an ingenious plan of so trimming the petticoat that it serves to give the desired fashionable effect to the dress, by keeping it out at the back. Our diagram is the model for the best of these petticoats that has yet been devised. The pattern consists of four pieces. No. 1—Half of the Back Breadth. No. 2—Half of the Side-Breadth. No. 3—Half of the Bustle. No. 4—Half of the lowest Flounce. The pieces may easily be distinguished by the numbers on the diagram; and the back and side-breadths are placed just as they are to be joined together, as may be seen by the corresponding notches at the top. The dotted lines on the half of the bustle show where the casings are to be put for the steels. The bustle should have perpendicular as well as horizontal steels—five of the former, and three of the latter. The bustle meets in front below the waist, where it is fastened with three buttons; a string is added at each side, which when tied, makes more or less protuberance, as desired. We only give half of the lowest flounce, which is rounded on the front sides. The other flounces are graduated in width to suit the petticoat. It will be seen the petticoat has no front width; but the side-breadths are bordered at each side by four inch frill. The material may be either scarlet camlet, crinoline muslin, or brilliante. Any lady with the aid of this diagram, can make the petticoat.

* *

AUTHOR'S NOTE:

Cut section 3 on fold of material, mark the dash lines, and sew tape-covered boning to dash lines or stays. The boning is sewn to the lining part of petticoat so stitches do not show on the right side. These may be sewn on by hand or by machine. Follow directions given by "Peterson's".

Next sew buttons or snaps to front closing and cut a band to fit the bustle and doll's waist. Sew to bustle as shown in drawing.

Sew center back seam of piece 1; sew flounces, according to "Peterson's" directions to 1 using piece 4 as lower flounce, cutting double the size of piece 1 for fullness. Graduate each flounce as shown in drawing. Sew 2 to 1, matching notches. Line all. Sew a frill or ruche to section 2 as shown.

* * * * * * * * * * * * * * * * * * * *

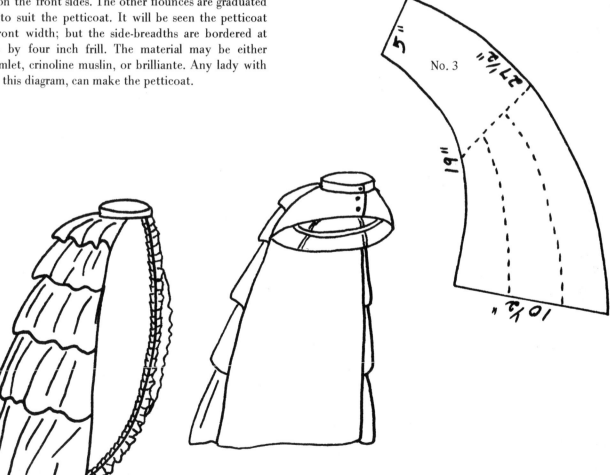

1870 PETERSON DIAGRAM PETTICOAT FOR SHORT DRESSES

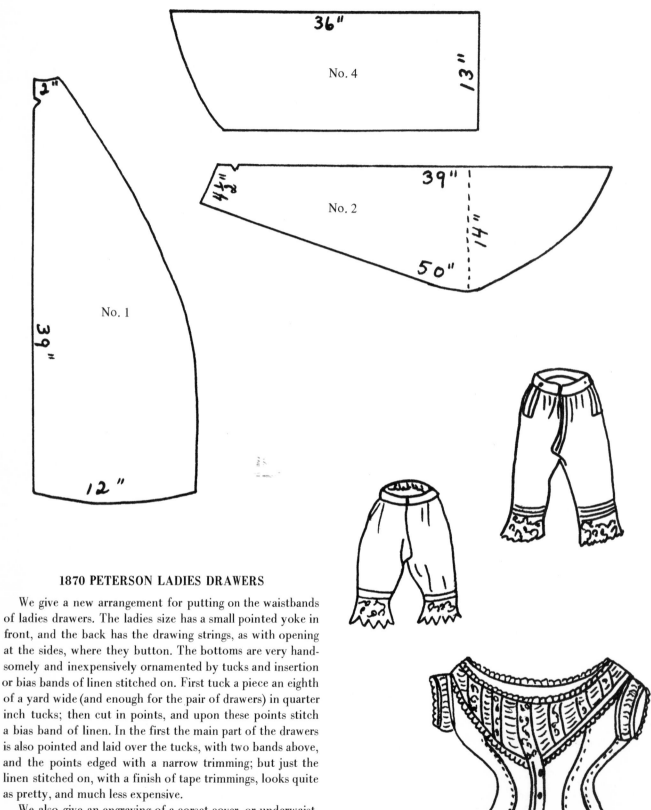

1870 PETERSON LADIES DRAWERS

We give a new arrangement for putting on the waistbands of ladies drawers. The ladies size has a small pointed yoke in front, and the back has the drawing strings, as with opening at the sides, where they button. The bottoms are very handsomely and inexpensively ornamented by tucks and insertion or bias bands of linen stitched on. First tuck a piece an eighth of a yard wide (and enough for the pair of drawers) in quarter inch tucks; then cut in points, and upon these points stitch a bias band of linen. In the first the main part of the drawers is also pointed and laid over the tucks, with two bands above, and the points edged with a narrow trimming; but just the linen stitched on, with a finish of tape trimmings, looks quite as pretty, and much less expensive.

We also give an engraving of a corset cover, or underwaist, for summer wear under thin dresses. It scarcely needs a description, as the design is so perfect; note puffs of nainsook between rows of insertion.

1870 PETERSON LADIES MORNING CAP

This cap is to be made of white Swiss muslin, trimming with a ruche of the same bound with a narrow, colored ribbon. We give a diagram also, with half of the crown of the cap.

The pointed piece goes on the front, and the crown is gathered into it; the pointed part comes over the forehead, and the part of the crown from B to C is gathered into the little band eight inches long and one inch and a half wide. Trim the whole with a quilling and add a bow on the top. This cap, although called a morning cap, is quite suitable for home wear all day.

1870 PETERSON PATTERN FOR AN ALL-ROUND SKIRT
(FITS 10" MANNIKIN DOLLS)

As All-Round skirts are now so universally worn, a pattern of one will be found useful to subscribers. These skirts are now trimmed in various ways, the newest style being a flounce from twelve to sixteen inches in depth, according to the height of the wearer. If the flounce is plaited, the folds all fall in the same direction in the Russian style; if gathered under, a heading or a ruche is added to the flounce.

Our pattern consists of four pieces: Half of front breadth, two side breadths, and half of back breadth. The order in which the pieces join will be known by the notches on the side of the diagram, which must correspond. The front breadth has a single notch on the side on which it joins to the next breadth. The back breadth has three notches. The two front breadths are sewn plain to the waistband if the figure is slight, but they must be somewhat eased should the figure be stout. The remaining breadths are gathered. It has recently become fashionable to wear a train-skirt over a short All-Round one, and the style of the newest creation is given in the accompanying illustration. This train, which can be slipped on and off at pleasure, imparts a very dressy appearance to the toilet for either indoor or outdoor wear. By the aid of this diagram, most ladies can make the skirt themselves.

* *
AUTHOR'S NOTE:

Follow directions as previously given and trim to accomodate the bodice and tunic. Cut waistband to fit doll's waist. Sew onto skirt allowing for closing. Attach hook and eye. This skirt may be used for the bodice and panier tunic and the Chevalier Casaque. Also, the dress shown with skirt can be adapted by using Chevalier Casaque and rounding out the revers to make the necessary shaping. A train can easily be made to create the fashion shown in drawing.

* *

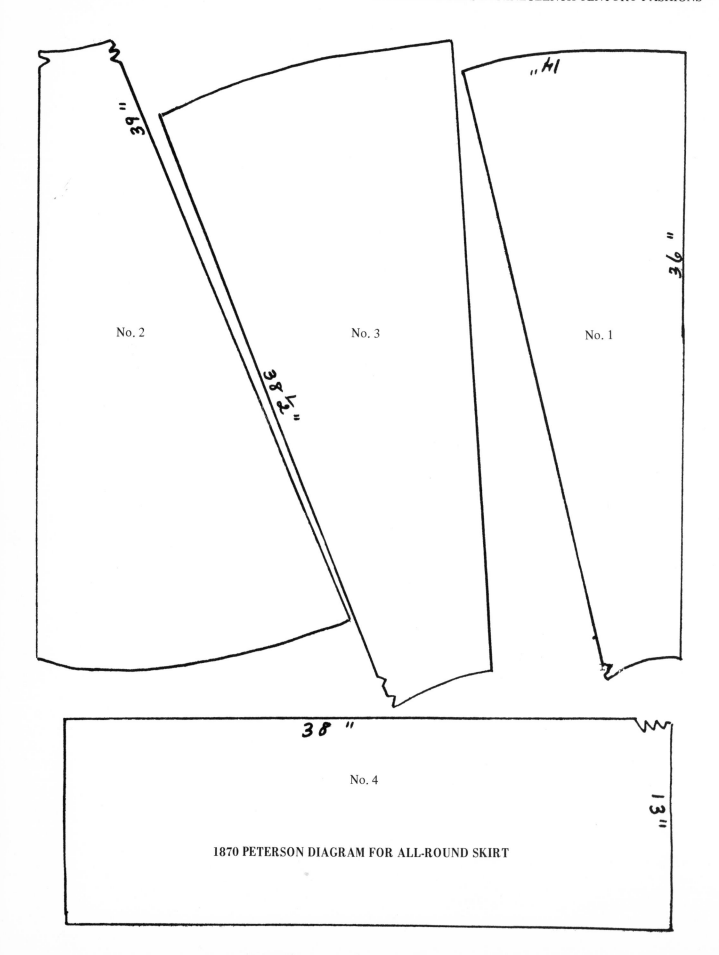

No. 2

No. 3

No. 1

39 "

41 "

36 "

38½"

No. 4

38 "

13 "

1870 PETERSON DIAGRAM FOR ALL-ROUND SKIRT

ROSETTE CAP 1870 PETERSON

We give an engraving of a cap. This cap will be very suitable for a dress cap, either for dinner or small evening party for ladies who are accustomed to wearing some sort of headdress. Being very simple, almost any lady can make it for herself. A small piece of foundation lace is gathered pretty full, two rows, then dispose of some loops of black velvet ribbon an inch and a half broad, on which add a small rosette of narrow lace. Two long loops of the velvet graduating with small rosettes, fall over the hair at the back; also two floating ends of the lace sewn together are added at both sides. Four yards of the wide blonde lace will be required, and five yards of the narrower width, with three yards of velvet ribbon.

* *

AUTHOR'S NOTE:

This rosette cap will work up beautifully for your doll. It is simple to copy by gathering lace to simulate the drawing.

* *

A USEFUL CRINOLINE OF 1871 PETERSON

(FITS 10" MANNIKIN DOLLS)

Here is the most useful crinoline that has come under our notice, as by simply changing the flounce, it can be made available for either an ordinary costume or an evening toilet. We give also, on the next page, a diagram. The portion represented comprises the upper part, and there are five pieces which represent one half of it. These pieces are front, back, two pieces for fastening the elastic straps to, and the band. They may be distinguished thus: The front has one notch, and is plain, the back (which is to be joined to it) has seven pricked horizontal lines; these indicate the position of the steels; the smaller of the two triangular pieces is joined to the top by one notch, the larger by two notches. Elastic straps are to be sewn to each of these pieces, and they fasten to the corresponding straps on the other side with sliding buckles. The belt is made with drawing strings at the back, plain in front, and fastening with a button. To the pattern here given a flounce is to be added. This flounce should measure four yards fourteen inches in width, and eighteen inches in depth, terminating with a hem of five inches. It is gathered into a band the width of the skirt and has buttonholes about finger apart, the buttons being sewn on the line which marks the

second steel. The flounce can therefore be taken off and washed when needed, without the upper part coming to pieces. The material of the model petticoat is white brilliante, but scarlet camlet for the upper part, and a white startched flounce for the lower also would answer. Both an inside and outside view is given.

* *

AUTHOR'S NOTE:

Cut pieces of diagram placing all on double material. Line pieces 3, 4, and 2 front; sew center back seams marking the dash lines for gathering and placing tapes for bones. Narrow strips may be cut from a plastic bottle or boning may be purchased in fabric shops for this purpose. Cut two waistbands, one for lining, leaving inner band open a little for the drawstrings. Sew pieces 3 and 4 to the left side of crinoline as shown in drawing. Seam front to right side of gathered crinoline as shown. Stitch band to petticoat. Sew button or snap on center front and run drawstring through band. Add a flounce as described to the lower part, making flounce twice the width of petticoat and of required length.

* *

DIAGRAM PATTERN FOR A USEFUL CRINOLINE
1871 PETERSON

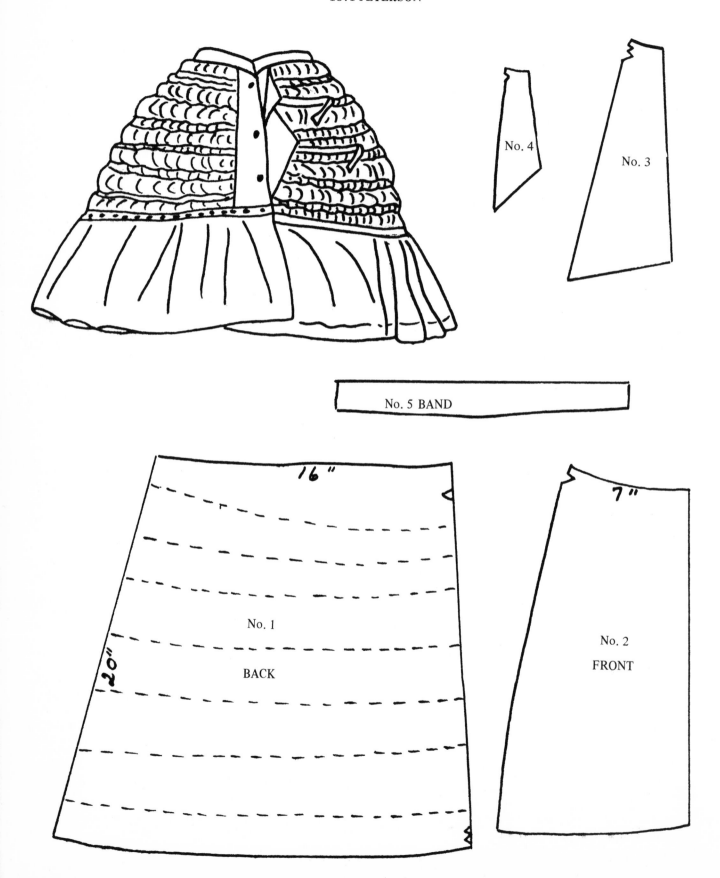

1871 PETERSON
PANNIER AND DIAGRAM TO FORM PALETOT
(FITS 10½" HIGH HEEL FIGURE DOLLS)

We give here an engraving of a pannier, with which to form a paletot, and also diagrams by which to cut it out. The pannier may be made of the same material as the dress or of cashmere or silk, if preferred. These diagrams must be enlarged of course; the size, in inches, is marked on each. We think that with these directions any lady can make the pannier herself, and so get up a very stylish costume, at comparatively small expense. It is trimmed with black lace over a band of white silk.

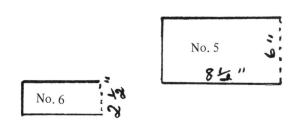

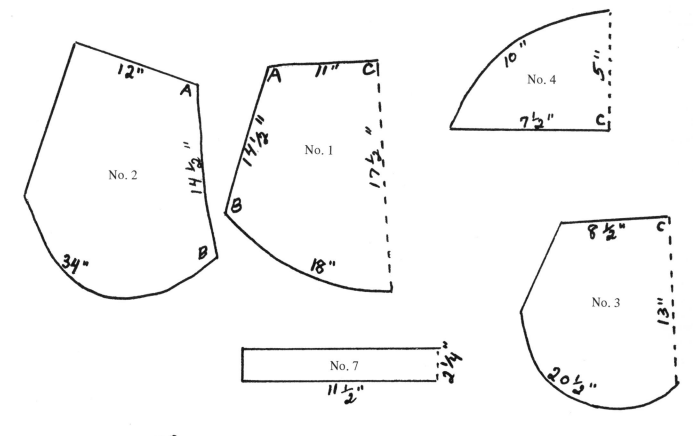

* *

AUTHOR'S NOTE:

Sew A-B to A-B front and back, pieces 1 and 2. Line piece 3 and attach ruche to edge, sew to back matching C. Line panniers. Sew on band, plaiting pieces 1 and 2 to fit band as shown in drawing. Sew hook and eye for closing on band. Trim pannier front and lower part with same ruching. Add ruche to piece 4, line and plait in fan-shape. Ruche and line piece 5 bow, make a plait and catch to C on fan piece. Cut two No. 6 pieces and line, wrap around fan-shaped bow as shown and sew all together. Attach snaps to band and fan-bow and snap in place on band. The ruching may be made of lace or any other suitable material to match the costume.

* *

1871 PETERSON PARIS PALETOT
(FITS 10" DOLLS)

We give here an engraving of a new Paletot, called "Paris Paletot" on account of its style, it is made of twilled reps, and is trimmed with velvet. We also add a diagram by which to cut it out. Nos. 2 and 3 are really only one piece, being cut together.

This paletot is straight in front and slightly fitting to the figure. It is trimmed with velvet, cut on the bias, and cut out in graduated scallops at the edge. Two large buttons are placed at the back. The paletot is fastened in front with large velvet buttons.

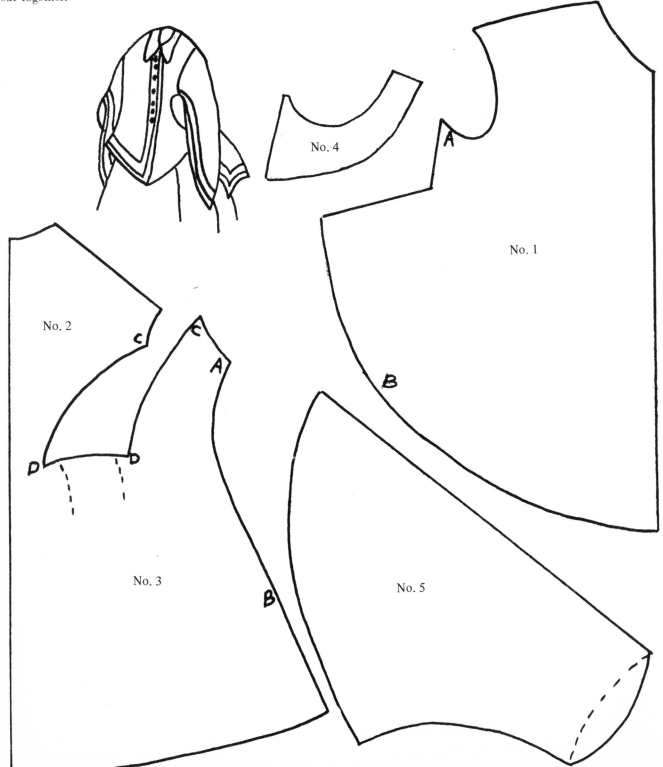

ON NEW BASQUE BODICE

at the back and one point on each hip. In front it fastens to the waist with buttons; from there it diverges at each side and forms a point. The sleeve is a pagoda form; it is box-plaited at the elbow and the frill falls with the point. It can be trimmed with fringe, gimp, or velvet. Our model is of black silk, ornamented with buff lace, headed by a full silk ruche.

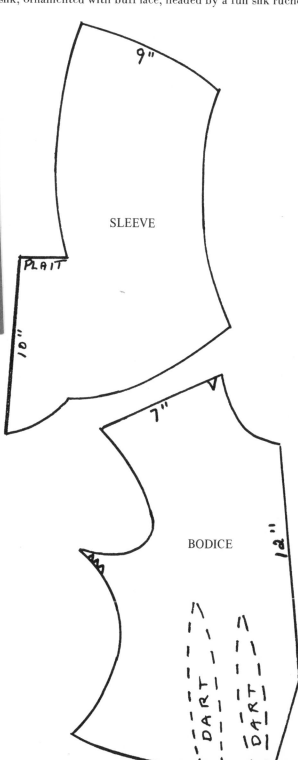

1871 PETERSON NEW BASQUE BODICE

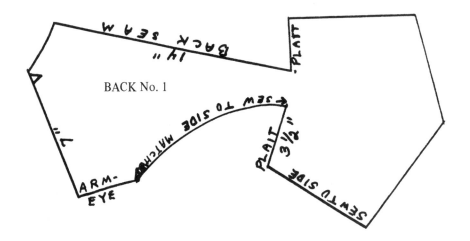

* *

AUTHOR'S NOTE:

REPRODUCTION OF AN 1871 DRESS

In October, 1971, I was invited to participate in a local "Heritage Day" event. Not being fortunate enough to own an original nineteenth century dress, I did the next best thing by enlarging a diagram from Peterson's. I chose an 1871 diagram thus spanning a hundred years.

Three fortunate ladies who attended the celebration owned original nineteenth century dresses which had belonged to their grandmothers. It was a treat for me to see these original gowns modeled by these women who were in their eighties and nineties. One lady wore a lovely black lace fichu which dated back to the 1860s.

To prepare a pattern for my copy of the 1871 dress I enlarged the diagram on brown paper bags, cut open and laid flat. I first measured the shoulder line given in inches and drew it on the paper bag, then shaped the armhole and other pieces. I was quite surprised to see how easily the lines matched.

The dress uses seven and one-half yards of forty-five inch material. One and one-half yards of taffeta of a contrasting color for the ruching is cut in four-inch widths the length of the material and pinked on both edges. These strips are joined together, folded from each edge to the center, stitched down, and then box-pleated to make the ruching. A black cord is handstitched in the center of the ruching to hide the machine sewing.

The skirt is gathered at the waistline with a set-in band, then a flounce, cut double the width of the skirt to assure fullness, is added to the skirt.

The tunic overskirt is also set in a band and lace trims the tunic and sleeve edges. Self-covered buttons on the bodice front complete a very authentic dress. Instead, you may wish to use the panier diagram of 1871 shown elsewhere in this volume. My dress took two weeks to complete.

The large circular pin worn at the neckline is my International Doll Club Association pin made by Olive Brunson. The pin seems to belong on this dress.

The diagrams in this book are excellent for enlarging to full size for centennials and local events such as the one in which I participated. The diagrams as given will fit Barbie dolls; notice the Barbie in my left hand in the picture.

* *

1872 PETERSON INFANTS SHOE

We give a pattern full size, for an infant's shoe in braiding.
We add here, two designs for infants' quilted boots. These
boots may be made in silk, satin, or pique.

JULY 1876 DELINEATOR MAGAZINE

MATERIALS: Camel's-hair goods continue to be the most stylish fabrics in woolens, and though the number of widely differing materials coming under that head is very great, the name remains the same, differing neither with the season, nor the texture or quality of the goods. Sometimes it is modified by an adjective, as, for instance, in canvas camel's-hair, which is woven to represent meshes of embroidery canvas, and when made up into overdresses resembles the basket silk now so fashionable.

Plain colors predominate, and the dark shades tend toward the invisable, while a large number of the light goods are displayed in ecru tints. When entire costumes are selected, striped goods are frequently chosen for the overskirt and basque, or polonaise, while the dress skirt and sleeves are made of the plain material, both varieties however, mingling in the trimming. In such instances the contrast is not striking as the groundwork of the striped fabric harmonizes in color with the plain goods, and the stripes are either of uniform or varying shades of the same color. If the costume is to be all of the same material, dark goods of solid or very indistinct mixed colors are chosen. Although silk is just as fashionable as ever for combination with such suits, it is no longer considered indispensable to a stylish costume, as the contrast may be rendered fully as harmonious and agreeable without its aid, and the weight of fine summer camel's-hair is no greater than the most expensive French cashmere.

A fabric called "lace camel's-hair" has recently been introduced for overdresses, the leading colors being ecru, brown, and drab. The open spaces are about as large and as close together as the meshes of loosely woven grenadine, and the wool consists of a soft heavy thread which is so firmly entwined with the finer warp as to leave no room for displacement. It is all wool, and is of double width, while the price is very reasonable.

Cashmere, Empress cloths, and Alpacas preserve the even tenor of their way, varying but slightly from their standard prices, and following the lead of silks and camel's-hair goods in colors.

There is a medium class of worsted, and mixed cotton and worsted goods, which deserves special mention, though it would be hard to classify the species under any other head than that of suitings. There are many varieties, none having any distinctive name, though some of the more pronounced bear a strong likeness to other well known fabrics. For instance, we have before us a sample composed of worsted and hard twisted cotton, and having a lustrous silky finish. The color is drab plaided with lines of a darker shade, and the piece displays a marked similarity of fine mohair. It is however, about thirty five percent cheaper than mohair, though the difference in value could scarcely be detected by a casual observer. It is made up either alone or in connection with plain goods of the same color, and with the addition of appropriate trimmings constitutes a very pretty costume.

Another of these nondescript fabrics has a plain stripe of a dark shade, and a second stripe formed of several hairlines of different shades of the same color, the entire surface being brocaded with the darker tint. This style is similar to the heavy silk-faced brocades, and is largely used with plain goods matching the darker stripe.

Another fabric, which is quite stylish at the present time, is pongee finely checked upon white with comparatively wide lines of either blue, brown, or black, set closely together. It is made up into polonaises, basques and overskirts, or entire suits, and is also frequently combined with plain Alpaca and Empress cloth matching the dark check. The prices have the full range of plain pongee, but for actual wear the checked variety is the most desirable.

As predicted by us some time ago, old fashioned bareges have been restored to the ranks of fashion, and are now quite popular with those who desire light, airy garments. They are shown principally in white with dark stripes, and by many are preferred to grenadines, this fact being perhaps attributed to the difference in price.

Cambrics and English Cheviots are seen chiefly in broken patterns and mixed colors, and will be made up more extensively for street wear than has been observable at this season for many years past.

'Centennialisms' creep out in various ways, and make themselves felt even in the realms of fashion.

Bunting, hitherto chiefly known as a material for flags, is now displayed as a dress fabric, and has been reduced sixty-five percent in price. Either blue or white would look very well in a dress, but not even the possession of an unusual amount of patriotism could in our estimation render the brilliant red suitable for such purposes. The first two tints are fashionable for seaside or mountain costumes, and by the addition of snowy lingerie and knots of ribbon, the contrast peculiar to the American "colors" might be agreeably brought out.

Smoked-blue, dun-gray and Abyssinian brown are the leading shades in plain silks, while in striped goods no change is noticable.

Damasse silks in blue, pink, brown, drab, and the numerous shades of ecru, are the most fashionable for elegant evening overdresses, and in viewing these goods we are in admiration of the artistic conceptions of the manufacturer. The colors are toned down to most exquisitely delicate tints, and the varying effects produced upon them by light and shade are beautiful to behold. One sample of pale ecru has a somewhat heavier stripe of a slightly deeper hue, and the two tints unite to form the brocaded pattern. The lighter appearing on the darker and vice-versa. Another has a silver ground broken by leaves and flowers outlined by a raised thread of blue.

Hamburg and guipure net are not new names, but the goods are fully as fashionable as they were a year ago, and are cheaper, as is frequently the case with materials which have enjoyed continuous popularity from one season to another. Hamburg net, may be laundered without losing its fresh, new appearance, if sufficient care is exercised.

TRIMMINGS

Midsummer, the season for dainty fabrics and trimmings, has again returned, with its usual array of light draperies and attractive ornaments.

As incidentally mentioned in a previous issue, organdies and lawns now come with bordered edges; one band being wider than the other, though the two present the same design. Sometimes the border, though attached to a lawn having a pure white ground covered with delicate twigs, leaves, or blossoms, is a bewildering continuation of gorgeous colors whose bright hues are softened by the transparency of the fabric. Brilliant blossoms, variegated foliage and bright buds twine about each other in charming variety, and when applied to the costume, wreathe it with garlands as attractive as they are fanciful. Other borders belonging to fabrics of tinted patterns are in lace designs, and some of them are exquisite imitations of French lace. In applying trimming of this description there are many methods that may be pursued. One lady will prefer it put on as a ruffle, which must be gathered by a cord run in a shirr at or near the top. Another will use it upon ruffles or flounces, sewing it to the lower edge of each, turning it up on the outside and stitching it to position. This arrangement will of course more perfectly show the pattern, but whether it is as graceful as the other is a question for individual decision. Again, when there is sufficient, such bordering looks very pretty laid in side-plaits, and used upon the bottom of the basque and overskirt, and also as an edging to a flounce. In preparing the borderings, they should be separated from the material before the garment is cut out, and in such a manner that enough of the fabric is left below as well as above the design for hems or seams. These three methods seem to be the most appropriate for borderings. Prints, cambrics and percales are also trimmed in this manner, being in many instances provided with pretty borders which seldom present any other color than those making up the design of the center portion of the width.

Returning to lawns and organdies, we find many costumes of these two fabrics prettily trimmed with the material in instances where no borders accompany the patterns; plaitings, shirrings and ruffles being used in a majority of cases. An additional finish is often given to ruffles by joining to the bottom, either with the hems or by an over-hand stitch, tiny edgings of Italian Valenciennes, a lace lately much employed for lingerie, and in trimming undergarments and finishing suits and overdresses of sheer white goods. In fact, so closely does the imitation resemble the real Valenciennes in many instances, that it becomes quite a puzzle even to the connoisseur to detect the differences. For elaborate white overdresses, this lace is used in widths ranging from one to two inches; insertion, with puffs of the material, making up the main portions, and the edging being used as a finish. The arrangement of the insertion and puffs is always alternate, and generally perpendicular, though in some instances they form a point at the center of the front and back of the garment and occasionally extend across the front diagonally. Sometimes this lace is used with strips of velvet or of watered silk or ribbon in delicate tints, and a wide frill of the edging is employed to complete the garment. Tuckings are also in a variety of ways. For thin white goods, the effect is prettier if they are bias, and the proper way to make them so, is to tuck a width of cloth and then cut it in bias strips of the desired width. These strips may be applied in any of the outlines in which bias bands or folds are arranged, and, after the edges are confined by tiny bias bands of the goods, the material may be cut from under the tucking, thus rendering the trimming more effective. Valenciennes lace is also used in connection with this style of trimming.

For thicker white goods, such as lawn, nainsook, and cambric, Hamburg edgings are abundantly used, and as they are not only handsome but comparatively inexpensive, their popularity is, as it has long been, assured.

In addition to fringes for heavier goods there has appeared a trimming which is neither fringe nor lace, though it appropriates the materials of the former and weaves them into the patterns of the latter trimming. It is suitable for silk, cashmere, grenadine, or any black or dark-colored fabric of similar nature, and is called "passementerie", probably from a dearth of names in the word-mint of dry goods establishments, for there is no similarity between it and the trimming usually known under that name. Another trimming apparently relative of the first, is a heavy silk embroidery on black gauze, which looks as if it might be to black thin dresses what Hamburg embroidery is to those previously mentioned. Aside from these two, there appear to be no novelties, unless we include the armies of buttons which seem to make an encampment on every lady's dress. To be sure, buttons are not new, and have been used from time immemorial; but it is doubtful if they ever reaped a greater harvest for their manufactures than they are gathering at present. Those from a quarter to a half-inch in diameter are selected, and of such a color as will harmonize or directly contrast with the dress. Sometimes as many as four rows are placed down the closing edges of a basque or polonaise, each coming exactly opposite the other, or directly between two of the next row. A charming appearance is obtained by three rows arranged as last suggested. By referring to the engravings in the present issue of the "Delineator", it will be observed that polonaises as well as basques are being closed in the back, and that in this event one row of very small buttons is generally selected. Such an arrangement is unquestionably handsome, and it consequently finds a very general, though not an exclusive adoption. The effect is certainly very elegant; but as intimated above, the use of one, three, or four rows depends wholly on the taste.

MILLINERY

Walking hats are now being worn, that turn up at one side and are plain at the other, instead of rolling at both sides in the English style. English turbans are being very generally adopted, and to some are decidedly becoming. The 'Shepherdess' is also a pretty street hat, and is a cross between the

English walking hat and the ordinary flat style, the brim rolling only slightly at each side, and dropping low at the front and back of the round crown. It is predicted that 'Cavalier' hats will be introduced again in the fall, but as this appears to be only an indefinite rumor, too much dependence must not be placed upon it.

Ostrich tips are being more and more used, although their proper season has passed. As ever, they add to a hat at least as much style as any amount of blossoms, and in the long run cost less, and are always genteel and becoming. A single full tip, or two small ones, may be made to trim up a hat very prettily in connection with silk.

The trimming to all hats is grouped over the crown, though principally at the back; and quite as many hats are seen without ends as with them. In fact, those without ends seem to obtain the preference with many, and they certainly present a very stylish appearance.

Considerable shell pink is being used in preference to cream and ecru, these colors having been worn so long, and the variation being so agreeable, as well as becoming to many complexions that cannot bear the close proximity of white or yellow tints.

1876 DELINEATOR LADIES PROMENADE COSTUME

A novel feature at present appearing in costumes is apparently destined to meet with decided success. It consists wholly in the style of the overgarments, which close at the back, and either basques and overskirts, or polonaises. The engraving illustrates a suit, which includes a polonaise buttoned at the back, and is composed of silk and camel's-hair, with silk and velvet for trimmings. The skirt was cut by one of our latest patterns, and has a front gore, two gores at each side and a back breadth. The skirt is lined, and before being joined to the belt has a small plait laid over the seam of the front and side front gores, while the top of the back breadth and most of that of the side back gore are evenly gathered; this arrangement together with the shape of the gores, causing the greater portion of the fullness to fall at the back, where it remains without requiring assistance of the customary tapes. These, however, may be added to the seams joining the side gores, and tied across the back in the ordinary manner, should the wearer prefer a very close arrangement of her skirt drapery. The material of the skirt is silk of a very lustrous variety known as glace, which when made up into trimmings has a brilliant and sheeny effect; the curves and indentations giving it, as in the engraving, a lighter appearance than the plain surface presents. The bottom of the skirt is finished with a ruffle of the silk cut bias and narrowly hemmed at each edge. It is gathered near the upper edge to form a tiny ruffle, which serves as a dainty heading, and is set on so that its lower edge is even with that of the skirt. Above this ruffle is a second trimming, which though similarly arranged, includes these distinctive features - a frill, a puff, and a tiny standing ruffle -

and is in consequence considerably wider than the trimming at the bottom. A gathering thread is inserted near the upper edge, while a second is placed near the center of the strip. These two threads produce the features above mentioned, and in setting the trimming on the skirt they were placed sufficiently close together to give a very slight roundness to the puff formed between them. Both lines of gathering are caught to the skirt, while the frill falls from the lower edge of the puff in soft and pretty waves. Strictly speaking, the trimming

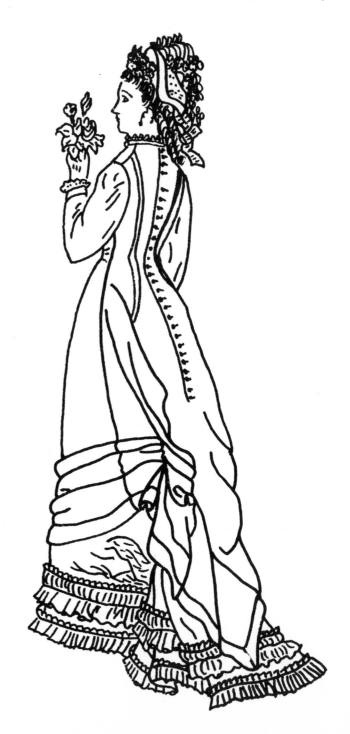

1876 DELINEATOR LADIES PROMENADE COSTUME

just described cannot be classed as shirring, since but one line of gathers is used in dividing it into the decorations mentioned. In the 'Work-Table' department of the present issue full instructions for making shirred trimmings together with a number of illustrations of the same, are presented; and any of the styles referred to therein could be successfully applied to the skirt of this costume, should they be preferred to the trimming represented. A decided preference seems to be given to narrow skirt trimmings, the popular width not exceeding ten inches, whether composed of one or more ruffles or plaitings. Box-plaited flounces have once more returned to favor for silk dresses, and they may be bordered with narrow shirred or plaited trimmings, or finished with facings blindstitched to position. The pattern used for the skirt is appropriate for any material and may be employed for cambrics, prints, lawns, cashmeres, Alpines, brilliantines, or velvet, as well as for the goods represented.

The overdress displays all the prevailing characteristics of its kind, and is both charming and stylish. The front is fitted at each side by two darts and a cross-basque seam, each curved closely to the figure and contributing equally to the adjustment. Its skirt is deep and rounding, and the effect illustrated results from the arrangement of the drapery, which will be described further on. The back is fitted at each side by a side back extending to the shoulder, and closes from the neck to quite a distance below the waistline with buttonholes and tiny velvet buttons; the fold formed below the closing by the hem of the overlapping side being tapered to a point and confined by a continuation of the buttons. As the back is cut without a seam at the center, the underlapping side of the opening is faced with a strip of the material, thus making the fold less bulky than it would otherwise be, and greatly aiding in a smooth disposal of it. Near the bottom of each side back skirt, three plaits turning upward on the outside are made, and beneath them tapes are fastened and then tied across the back to draw the front into the pretty folds illustrated. Nearly opposite the plaits the side back seam is caught up on the underside, thus adding another fold to the drapery and affording sufficient puffiness to the back. This polonaise is made of camel's-hair of an ecru tint, and the bottom is bordered with a band of velvet, blindstitched to position in its upper edge. The neck, the side back seams, the arms'-eyes, and the overlapping edge of the opening at the back, are prettily corded with velvet. The sleeves are cut from silk, but in order to preserve the harmony of the costume, each are finished at the wrist with a velvet band a trifle narrower than that on the bottom of the polonaise. Crepe lisse ruching completes the neck and wrists, its softness lending a pleasing delicacy to the complexion. The pattern used in cutting the polonaise is No. 4469, price is 6d. Sterling or 35 cents, and is suitable for any fabric used for such garments. A variety of materials, from those of diaphanous texture to heavy velvets, are represented by polonaises of this description, while the more practical de beges, shepherds' check, and fine serges are also frequently adopted for this style of garment. Sometimes the edges are scalloped, slashed, or blocked, and bound with velvet or silk;

or they may be bordered with a plaiting or a shirred ruffle. On garments of a particularly rich quality, fringes and laces are employed with a superb effect, especially if headed by any of the new gimps, passementeries, or moss trimmings. Some of the most stylish garments, however, are utterly devoid of trimming, except on the sleeve and neck, the effect apparently depending wholly on the drapery.

The hat is of white chip, with a square crown and undulating brim. The crown is encircled by a twist of soft silk, white loops of the same are placed above the twist at the front, and gracefully mingle with a heavy spray of fine blossoms, which fall over the crown and at the back of the hat above short ends of ribbon.

1876 DELINEATOR LADIES POLONAISE
BUTTONED AT BACK

The fancy for garments buttoned at the back grows stronger as the season advances, and many of the most fashionable polonaises for summer are made in this way, one very becoming shape being illustrated in these engravings. The materials used in the formation of the garment are gray de bege and black silk, the silk being used for the sleeves and trimming. Long curved darts of nearly equal lengths, together with the cross-basque seams, adjust the front smoothly to the figure; but the back is gored, having narrow side forms which extend to the shoulder seams and produce the slender, long waisted appearance now so much in vogue. The skirt portions of both back and front are deepest in the center and curve upward slightly toward the side seams, so that when the garment is draped a strikingly graceful outline is produced, the entire lower edge being finished with a cording of silk. A cord is also inserted in the side back and arms'-eye seams. The back of the garment is cut on a fold of the material, and the opening, which extends quite a distance below the waistline, has one side turned under in a hem for the buttonholes, while the other, upon which tiny braid buttons are placed very closely together, has a facing. At the termination of the opening the lap is firmly tacked, and below this is reduced in width, being tapered to a point beneath a continuation of the line of buttons closing the garment. The narrow coat sleeve has considerable fullness allowed at the highest part of the top, so that it will fit nicely, as the shoulder of the body is quite short; the under portion of the sleeve is narrower than the upper and is sewed in nearly plain. A cord of the silk completes the neck, this simple method affording abundant opportunity for different styles of neck dressing and other arrangements of trimming. The drapery is particularly effective, but is easily arranged. Three upward turned plaits are laid low down in the skirt a few inches back of each side seam, and beneath them tapes are sewed. Nearly opposite these clusters a single plait is made in the side back seams, and the parts are afterward brought together beneath the back and firmly tacked; the tapes are then tied together and the front of the skirt is arranged in three broken folds. This style of drapery is particularly effective, and in exact conformity to the bustles worn at the present time, which are constructed to make the hips appear small and throw all the fullness backward to the bottom of the skirt.

Garments of this style have a youthful, attractive appearance, and are very becoming to stout figures. We have the pattern in thirteen sizes for ladies from twenty-eight to forty-six inches, bust measurements. Six and one-fourth yards of material, twenty-seven inches wide, together with a yard and one-fourth of silk, twenty inches wide, are needed in making the garment illustrated, for a lady of medium size.

THE WORK TABLE FLOUNCES
1876 DELINEATOR

So various are the means employed to trim dresses with material, that a whole magazine would scarcely afford room enough to describe them; but a chapter now and then will surely suffice to provide our readers with the latest ideas in the arrangement and disposal of the leading methods. Among the prettiest may be mentioned shirred trimmings, which are obtaining a wide popularity. There are a variety of ways in which the edges of shirred ruffles or flounces may be completed, some of which are illustrated by the pictures.

Figure No. 1 represents a prevailing style of finish, and one that is easily accomplished. The flounce is cut bias and about half a yard deep, and is then hemmed at the top with the machine, or if preferred, or more convenient, it may be done by hand. The lower edge is turned up on the outside for about an inch, and simulates a facing, being blindstitched to position. As shirred trimmings are always cut bias, this arrangement will lie as smoothly as if a facing had been cut expressly for it and seamed on. In making the shirring the safest way is to mark where each gathering is to be inserted, to insure regularity. This may be done either with white or tinted French marking chalk according to the color of the goods. Although the illustration is small, it serves to show the relative distances of the shirrings from each other, as well as the space occupied by each line of shirring. The first line in the flounce being described is placed a little more than an inch from the top, and the two gatherings forming the shirring

are about three-fourths of an inch apart; the stitches being very fine and evenly made, and drawn so as to produce but comparatively slight fullness.

To make the flounce full in all portions, the surest method is to measure the skirt, or whatever garment is to be trimmed, and then allow one third of the measurement more, in the flounce; thus making the latter once and a third the length of the space it is to trim; then mark it, and the space also, into four equal sections; gather or shirr every quarter of the flounce separately, and make them each occupy just exactly one-quarter as it is shirred, but in the flounce having several shirrings the most convenient way will be to complete all the shirring and then add the flounce.

Owing to the arrangement of the design illustrated, the width of the first puff may be rather uncertain to the observer. It corresponds, however, with that of the second puff, the second line of shirring being just as far from the first as the third is from the second, and each line of shirring occupying the same space in width as the first one. The last puff is also identical in width with the other two while each is about four inches wide, and the frill falling below is about an inch wider than the puff.

When the flounce is set on the skirt, it will have to be drawn closer at the first and second shirrings than at the lower two, on account of the gores, which give every skirt a flaring shape. The first two, as well as the last two shirrings are

THE WORK TABLE FLOUNCES 1876 DELINEATOR

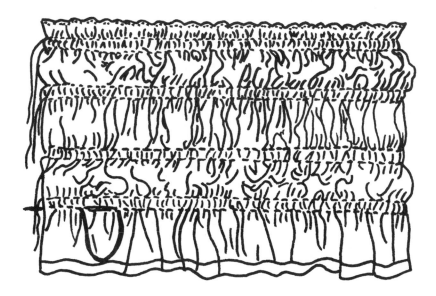

FIGURE NO. 1. - FLOUNCE WITH THREE PUFFS

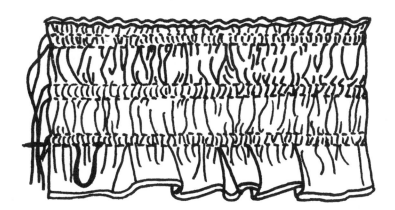

FIGURE NO. 2 - FLOUNCE WITH TWO STRAIGHT PUFFS

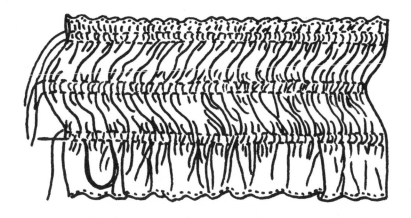

FIGURE NO. 3. - FLOUNCE WITH TWO DIAGONAL PUFFS

placed at least an inch or an inch and a half closer together than the second and third, so as to produce a full round puff at the center being as flat to the skirt as the fullness will permit.

As will be easily seen, the arrangement may be reversed or varied in other ways, and many methods of changing it will probably occur to the reader, especially if she has a taste for making trimming. Such being the case, she need not necessarily confine to the directions just given. For instance, she may prefer to finish the edges like those of figure No. 2, with a tiny hem blindstitched to position; or if her goods have a double surface, like silk, Alpaca, de bege or similar materials, the lower edge of the flounce may be hemmed by a machine, and the upper finished by a rolled hem like that at the top of the flounce illustrated by figure No. 3. Sometimes the heading is double, the top being turned down on the under side far enough to be secured by the shirring.

The flounce illustrated by figure No. 2 is arranged precisely like the one just described as far as the shirring and the relative width of the frill are concerned, but is finished at each edge with a narrow hem blindstitched to position. In setting it on the garment, the shirrings are placed the full width of each puff apart, so that both of the puffs are flat. In order that the fullness may not become disarranged, the flounce is secured to the garment at each gathering in every line of shirring. Should a lady prefer a separate heading to a gathered flounce, it would be easy to form one by the method described for the puffs; cutting a strip wide enough for one puff at each edge of the width of the one at the top of each flounce illustrated. The heading can be applied in the same style as the flounce, either flat or rounding, as preferred.

Figure No. 3 illustrates a different arrangement of a trimming shirred like the one illustrated by the second engraving. The edges are finished by one of the methods suggested in the description of figure No. 1: the top is narrowly rolled over on the outside, but is blindstitched from the underside so that it is round like a piping. The process requires some care at first, but soon becomes easy to the operator. The lower edge of the flounce is simply machine hemmed. In setting this decoration on the garment the outside shirrings are placed much nearer each than they should be if the puffs were to lie straight, in order to obtain sufficient fullness to draw the middle shirring in the style illustrated. As in the other instances, this flounce must be caught to the garment at each line of shirring - a process especially necessary in this method of arranging trimming. Sometimes a double thread is used in making the gatherings, but generally a single one of strong sewing silk is preferred, as it is quite as firm as a double one of cotton, and gives less trouble through knotting and breaking. The widths of flounces is a matter for personal decision, and may depend upon the quantity of material provided, or individual preference.

TO ENLARGE OR REDUCE A PATTERN
TAKEN FROM PETERSON MAGAZINE

As it would be impossible for us to cut our patterns to suit the needs of our thousands of subscribers, we will give some simple directions for reducing or enlarging a pattern, as the case may be, our patterns being cut of an average size. If, on measuring, you find the bodice pattern we have given too large for you, pin each part together, one edge just passing over the other flatly. Measure round the decreased pattern, and, if you find it still too large, continue to take it in a little more at every seam except those of the bust-plaits. Cut off half the overlapping portion of each edge. If the pattern is too full in the bust, it will improve the figure to fill up with small pads of wadding made in a circular form about four inches across. If the pattern is too small, place it on a piece of paper and pin closely at edges; cut, it with a margin of the paper pinned all round. Treat all four parts of the bodice pattern in the same manner, allowing equal addition to each. Do not add to the piece between the bust-plaits. If more fullness is required for the bust, cut a small piece away from each part of the bodice that joins to the strip between the bust-plaits.

BLACK VELVET CUIRASS BODICE.

1878 Peterson

1878 Peterson

DRESS FOR SUMMER: FRONT AND BACK.

1878 Peterson

DINNER DRESS.   NEW STYLE OF DRESSING THE HAIR: FRONT.

1878 Peterson

HOME DRESS OF SOFT WOOLEN MATERIAL. NEW STYLE OF DRESSING THE HAIR: BACK VIEW.

1878 Peterson

WRAPS FOR SPRING WEAR.

1878 Peterson

LOUIS XV. JACKET: FRONT AND BACK.

1878 Peterson

THE "PIEROTT" COLLAR AND CUFFS.   BONNET.

1878 Peterson

HOUSE DRESS—FRONT. BONNET.

1878 Peterson

NEW STYLE OF BLOUSE WAIST: BACK AND FRONT.

1878 Peterson

BACK AND FRONT OF WALKING DRESS.

1876 Peterson

FASHIONS FOR JULY, 1876.

Figure No. 2.—Ladies' Street Costume

1878 Peterson

AFTERNOON DRESS FOR SUMMER: BACK AND FRONT.

1878 Peterson

WALKING DRESS· FRONT AND BACK.

1878 Peterson

HOUSE DRESS: BACK AND FRONT.

1878 Peterson

AFTERNOON DRESS: BACK AND FRONT.

1878 Peterson

SHORT COSTUME FOR YOUNG LADY. WALKING DRESS OF ÉCRU LINEN.

1878 Peterson

HOUSE DRESS. STRAW BONNET.

1878 Peterson

NEW STYLE MANTILLA. LEGHORN BONNET. STRAW HAT.

1878 Peterson

HOUSE DRESS.   NEW STYLE FOR THE HAIR.

1878 Peterson

BACK AND FRONT OF SERGE COSTUME.

1878 Peterson

HOUSE DRESS—BACK.   WINTER HAT.

1878 Peterson

YOUNG GIRL'S DRESS. FAN.

1878 Peterson

ANOTHER NEW STYLE FOR COLLAR AND CUFFS. HAT.

1878 Peterson

HOUSE DRESS. WALKING DRESS.

A GLOSSARY OF NINETEENTH CENTURY TERMS

A

absinthe — a very faint tint of blue

abyssinian — a brown color

agrafe — a clasp, buckle, or hooks and eyes

aigrette — a plume or tuft of feathers, worn on the head, aigrette feathers are taken from the Egret bird

aiguilettes — ornamental loops or cord

alamode — another meaning for a glossy silk which was used in the nineteenth century

albatross cloth — a thin woolen material; substitute for mohair, with a slight crinkled look, caused by the twist of yarn

algerine cloth — woolen material

alpaca — a woolen material; substitute for mohair

alpine — another form of Norfolk jacket

Alsatian — a bow, etc.; the name is given by the Alsatian women of France

amaranth — a color of reddish-blue with a high or low brilliance shading from pink to purple

antique bodice — a long waisted bodice with a long pointed front

arm's eye — the armhole

armure — a silk or woolen material, whose weave resembles chained armour

astrakan or astrakhan — a curly piled fabric resembling imitation Persian lamb

atlas — another meaning for silk

aumoniere — a purse which hangs from a belt of the waistline

B

barege — a guaze-like material, of a mixture of silk and worsted or a cotton and worsted, a sheer material with a silky finish

basque — a tight fitting waist or an extension of the corsage below the waist

batiste — a fine cotton or linen material which is also a substitute for lawn

bayadere trimming — flat trimming woven in or sewn on dress material

beaver cloth — a heavy woolen material with a nap on both sides

bertha or berthe — a lace collar, also a cape-like collar

bishop sleeves — a wide sleeve, gathered at the wrist

blond or blonde — a silk lace the color of blonde hair; a color, reddish-yellow

bodice — the upper part of a dress

body — another meaning for waist or bodice

bouffant — a puffed out part of a dress

bouillonne — any shirred or gathered trimming, a puff, dressmaking

brace — a kind of bretelle

braid — to bind, trim, or braid like hair

brandenbourg — cords and tassels

breadth — width of material or skirt gores, etc.

bretelle — a strap-shaped trimming

brilliante — a cotton type material figured, and sometimes displaying colored designs

brilliantine — a dress material with a gloss on both sides

broched — brocaded fabric with a raised design

broderie Anglaise — embroidered eyelet-like material

Brussels lace — a lace with figures in the ground

bunting — a lightweight wool

burnous — a mantle or cloak, which was influenced by the Arabian cloak

bustle — an arrangement of different kinds of material and construction, which was worn to hold the dress away from the body at the back

C

cambric — a fine linen or cotton imitation of linen

camel's hair — a material made from the camel-hair

camlet — a fabric of satin weave made of camel's hair and angora wool

casaque — a close fitting jacket, which is buttoned up to the neck, and the skirt is trimmed with fringe or lace depending on style

cashmere — a soft woolen made of goat's hair from the Kashmir goats

castellated points — vandykes

cavalier sleeve — a sleeve full to the elbow and tight at the wrist

ceinture — a girdle for adorning the waist of a dress

centre — center

chale — a soft woolen and silk material

challis — a very lightweight wool and cotton mixture

chambray — a gingham material with a colored warp and white mixture filled in

chamois — soft leather made from chamois sheep

chausses — stockings

checques — checks

chemise — a loose undergarment

chemisette — a sleeveless undergarment, or a sleeveless bodice, which usually covers the neck, shoulders, and breast; also an ornamental part of a dress

chenille fringe — a tufted cord of silk, worsted, wool, or cotton

cheviot — twilled woolen fabric

China crepe — equivalent to crepe de chine

Chinoise — Chinese art decoration

chintz — a glazed cotton

Clotilde — a kind of veil for bonnet

coat sleeve — straight sleeve with a slight curve at the elbow

coeur — heart shape

coiffure — a headdress

col a revers — neckline with revers

collarette — a cape of lace, small collar, etc.

coques — a small ribbon loops or bows, used for hats, boas, and dresses

coquilles — ruching for dresses, hats, or neckwear, gathered full

corsage — another meaning for the waist of a dress bodice

corset cover — a stiff, hooked or laced undergarment

court train — a very long train

coutil — a fabric used for corsets

crape — something made in silk, wool, or cotton made crinkly

cravat — a neck decoration or necktie

crepe — crinkled material, as crape

crepe de chine — a fine silk sheer crepe material

crepe lisse — a very sheer fabric, feels like crepe

crepeline — a very thin material of silk, or silk and wool

creves — heart-shape

crinoline — a petticoat, or a stiff cloth formerly used for underskirts

curtains — decoration for skirt or garment to hang artistically on the body as a drapery

D

damasse silk — a kind of brocaded material

dark — a very dark shade of blue, approaching black

de bege — a light woolen material, also beige color

de laine — a light textured fabric mixed with wool and cotton

deux jupes — two skirts

diadem — an ornamental headband, a crown, etc.

drab — a kind of thick woolen cloth of dull brownish-yellow color

dress elevator — any one of a number of methods used to adjust the length of the skirt

duite cloth — a French word for pick of weft, any woven web of any sort to form a weave; a fabric texture; a material with a pile nap; a course Indian calico; etc.

dun gray — a very dark gray color

E

embonpoint — plumpness of person; also stoutness

empress cloth — a wool, or wool and cotton blend, resembles merino but not twilled

epaulette — ornamental shoulder piece

F

faille — a ribbed silk fabric of plain weave

festoon — to drape in curves

flannelette — a soft cotton with nap on one or both sides

flounce — a deep gathered or pleated frill or ruffle

fluting — a decoration of a lady's ruffle like very tiny waves

footing — the straight edge of lace by which it is sewed to another fabric, also a ruffle guide at the hem of dress to prevent wear of the dress

foulard — a silk with a satiny finish

fourragere — a braided cord

frizette — a curl for the hair, also a kind of curling tool

G

galloons — a narrow binding or trimming of rich materials, also fancy braid or tape

gauffered or gaufferings — a fluted or crimped ornamentation on the edge of material formed with a heated crimping or gaufre iron

gauntlet — gloves and a fancy cuff for a sleeve

gauze — a transparent, thin and light material made of silk, linen, or cotton

gimp — a narrow flat piece of fabric often stiffened with wire; wimple or trim

gipsy bonnet — a small flat bonnet only covering the crown

girdle — a cord or band encircling the waist and hips

glace — a smooth and glossy surface; of cloth, leather, etc.

gore — method of cutting the material in a pyramidal shape

grenadine — a sheer gauze, made of silk, wool, or cotton; good substitutes are very sheer lawn, voile, or batiste

groseille or grosielle — a gooseberry color

grosgrain — a fabric of silk with a dull finish, also a ribbed taffeta ribbon

guipure — a heavy lace with large pattern applied to many kinds of laces

H

Hamburg — a kind of embroidered edging

headdress — a gauze or flower wreath trimmed with feathers, flowers, etc., worn with evening dress; also a manner of dressing the hair

henrietta cloth — a fine woolen material which sometimes had a warp of silk, used for ladies dresses

hermosa — a yellowish-brown, between old-gold and pale brown

hernani — a thin silk or woolen material, looks like grenadine

I

Isabeau — a triangular-shaped sleeve wide at the bottom to show an undersleeve; also a one-piece dress with no waist-line seams

J

jabot — a cravat of lace

jaconet — a thin cotton material

jockey — a flat trimming applied over the shoulder of a dress

jupe — a loose jacket, tunic, or bodice

jupons — petticoats or underskirts

K

kerseymere — a lightweight coarse woolen material, made smooth or ribbed

L

lame — cloth with a metal thread

lappet — pendant from a headdress hanging at the sides or behind made plain, trimmed, or with lace

lawn — a very fine cotton or linen material

leghorn — a plaiting used for bonnets and hats, made from leghorn straw

Limerick lace — lace made in Limerick, Ireland, by embroidering a pattern on net

linsey woolsey — a material of linen and wool, or cotton and wool, a very coarse fabric

lozenge — a diamond shaped figure

M

macaroon — a dress trimming, also a very large button

magenta — green color with a tinge of blue

Maltese lace — a heavy bobbin lace usually of black or white silk

mantelet — a scarf-like cape with long ends

mantilla — a small mantle, deep at the back, long ends in front

mantua — a woman's cloak, worn about 1700

marseilles — a cotton material resembling pique

Mechlin lace — a dainty bobbin lace

merino — a soft woolen material made of sheeps wool

metalasse or metalisse — a material of silk or silk and wool, sometimes metallic

mohair — a material made from the hair of the angora goat; a soft woolen and a substitute for alpaca

moire — a watered silk or taffeta

moon on the lake — a pearl color

mouches — small curled ornaments for bonnets

moufflon — a material resembling sheepskin

mousequetaire cuffs — large, lacy cuff turned back on a sleeve

mousseline — a sheer material

mousseline de laine — a material of muslin and wool

mull — another meaning for sheer muslin, sheer voile, or sheer batiste (very sheer)

muslin — a very fine thin cotton which came from India; heavier muslin cottons were made in America

N

nainsook — a fine muslin

nun's veiling — a fine woolen material with a smooth finish

O

ondit — a piece of gossip or a vague rumor

organdy or organdie — a sheer muslin with a stiff finish Note: If organdy is washed and ironed out softly it will serve for mull, providing it is not the organdy that keeps its stiffness after washing.

overdress — an outer or upper dress

overskirt — an upperskirt, shorter than the dress, and sometimes draped

P

Pagoda sleeve — a funnel shaped sleeve arranged to show the inner sleeve or undersleeve

paletot — an outdoor jacket and a knee length coat loosely fitted

panier or pannier — an overskirt puffed or looped full on the sides and back

Pardessus — any outer garment of half or three-quarter length with sleeves shaped into the waist

passementerie — trimmings of braids, cords, beads, gold or silver tinsel, etc.

pekin — silk material with stripes or print

pelerine — a woman's cape with long ends hanging down in front

pelon — a smooth stiff cloth without a bias, used for facing garments and body

percale — a smooth closely woven cotton

plait — to fold as pleats, also to make braids

plastron — trimming for the front of a bodice, usually of a different material or lace, narrowing from the shoulders to the waist

plisse — gathering or plaiting

plisse crepe — a cotton

point d'esprit — a fine cotton net with a woven square dot

polonaise — a dress with an overskirt bunched behind and completely uncovering the underskirt

pomona — the color of a yellow green apple

pongee — a soft silken material of lightweight texture

poplin — a corded material of silk or worsted mixture

pouf — a puff

Q

quill — another word for ruffle or plaited ridges, also feathers

quilles — flutings and refers to quill

quilling — lace, ribbon, etc., fluted or folded in a way to resemble quills

R

redingote — a close-fitting dress, opening in front to reveal the underskirt, also made in princess style with revers and buttons down front; outer coat with long full skirt

Regina — darker mauve color

reps — material of silk, wool, or silk and wool with a ribbed surface

reticule — a lady's purse

revers — facings or borderings turned back on a garment, also a lapel

rouleaux — roll

ruche — frilled or plaited net, lace, silk, or material for trimming dresses

ruff — a frill for the neck attached to a collar; to ruffle

S

sack — loose gown or jacket

sacque — a loose fitting outer garment

scallop or scollop — to mark or cut the edge in scallops, suggestive of the edge of scallops

serge — a material made of twilled woolen

shirr or shirrings — a series of runnings which are drawn up in full gathers

solferino — deep-toned, brilliant peach color

sultane — antique red color

surplice — a robe of fur, also having the neckline extended over each shoulder, to the opposite hip with a crossing in the center of the bodice, or a surplice collar; also a loose garment

T

tablier — apron-like front

taffeta — a material of glossy finish, both with soft or stiff silken finish

talma — hood or poncho

tarletan or tarletane — a transparent muslin

tissue — sheer fabric

toilet or toilettes — costume, attire, etc.

torsade — a twisted cord, also a worked ornament

tournure — another term for bustle

tucking — a fold made in a garment

tulle or thulle — a silk net material used for veils, dresses, etc; the name derives from Tulle, France, where it was first produced

U

underskirt — a petticoat, also worn as a skirt under a polonaise

undersleeve — a sleeve worn under another and showing from the uppersleeve (check 1860s fashions, pagoda sleeves, etc.)

upperdress — a tunic or polonaise worn over an underskirt

V

Valenciennes lace — a type of fine bobbin lace having a square or diamond-shaped mesh

vandyke — to form points, vandyke-edge, etc.; broad deep collar or cape of fine linen and lace

velour — a material similar to velvet

velours de laine — having a pile like velvet

velvet — a material woven of silk or cotton with a short thick pile

velveteen — a heavy cotton velvet

vicuna cloth — a woolen material

visite — a wrap, worn to go visiting

volant — another term for a flounce

voluminous — very full folds in a dress, etc.

W

wadded — padded out with cotton or wool

waist — a bodice, also a girdle or belt for the waist

Watteau polonaise — an overdress looped up at the sides of the skirt, with a pleat from the neck to the hemline

weft — having threads that cross the warp

willow leaf green — a light yellowish shade of olive

X

Y

Z

zamore — a dark red with metallic reflections, almost like terra-cotta red

Zouave — a loose fitting jacket

BIBLIOGRAPHY

Godey's Lady's Book and Magazine, Louis A. Godey, Philadelphia, 1859, 1865.

Peterson's Magazine, Charles J. Peterson, Philadelphia, 1860, 1864, 1870-2.

Delineator Magazine, The, Butterick Publishing Co., London and New York, 1876.

NEW STYLE BODICE.

INDEX

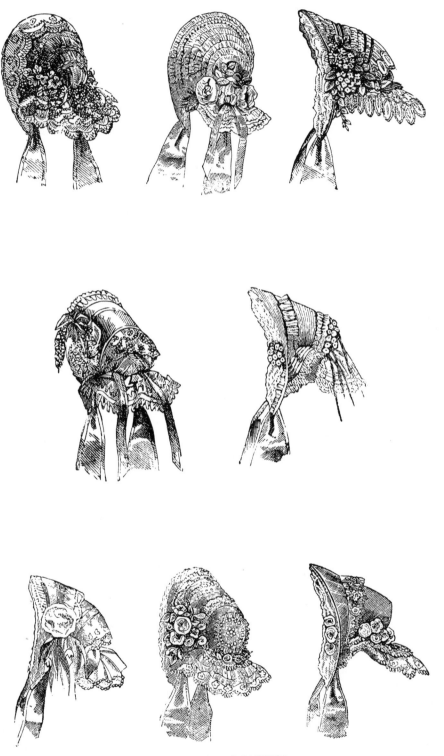

NEW STYLE OF BONNETS.

NOTES

NOTES